Simple Accountability

And Its Necessity In Your Life & Walk

Simple Accountability

And Its Necessity In Your Life & Walk

Dana Coverstone

Dedication

This book is dedicated to my wife Jennifer, and to my children, Keilah, Micah, and Hannah who have all made my life more accountable and blessed. My love for you can't be measured in words or actions because it is so much deeper than that.

Simple Accountability

Cover and Interior Layout by Uberwriters Christian Ghostwriters
www.uberwriters.com

Cover picture design by James Rader.

Unless otherwise indicated, scripture quotations are from the ESV® Bible (The Holy Bible, English Standard Version®), copyright © 2001 by Crossway, a publishing ministry of Good News Publishers. Used by permission. All rights reserved.

Scripture quotations marked (NLT) are taken from the Holy Bible, New Living Translation, copyright © 1996, 2004, 2015 by Tyndale House Foundation. Used by permission of Tyndale House Publishers, Inc., Carol Stream, Illinois 60188. All rights reserved.

ISBN 978-1-7379918-0-9 paperback

ISBN 978-1-7379918-1-6 eBook

Table of Contents

Appreciation

I am grateful for the many who reached out to me as a fifteen year-old teenager who was simply lost. I am even more thankful for those who have continued to help me improve my life spiritually. Pastors like Ernie Feasel and David Delp who mentored and invested in me as a teenager in their church, for Sam Bush, whom I served under for ten years and who led me with exceptional integrity. For the congregation of Jasonville Assembly of God who discipled me and steered me, both as a young man and as a staff pastor there. For Central Bible College professors who poured out and into me with knowledge and wisdom, and who prepared me for ministry. For the men at Living Word Ministries in Burkesville who have faithfully prayed with me for over ten years now. For the Assemblies of God who have been a solid and stable source of both doctrine and fellowship for over thirty years. For the men who I have prayed with over the years in several churches and for those who have been my active accountability partners for decades.

I am further extremely grateful for my wife and children who have made me laugh and cry and learn. And for my mom, Clara, who has been a great example of love, patience and understanding. I just hope she forgives me for some of the stories in this book she never knew about.

My hope, however, is in Jesus Christ who has taken me and shaken me, and walked with me through the fires of life, and kept me steady on the path He has for me. He keeps showing me things I never knew and keeps revealing Himself in ways I never understood. He is faithful and I praise Him for it.

Introduction

As a Bible College student I heard many messages on vision, church planting, success in ministry, and pretty much every new strategy you could imagine on building, growing, and developing churches and congregations. There were classes about service arrangement, building a worship team, the value of preaching in a series, expository preaching, and community outreach tips. There were classes for almost everything a church could do to impact the community in which it was planted. Add to that the countless district-ministry sessions where the latest, greatest, fad was paraded across the platform (with the book conveniently for sale in the foyer for only $19.95). It didn't take me long to realize these fads are not enough to sustain a leader. In fact, I believe they are the reason so many people in church leadership have lost their interest in fresh ministry ideas, with some even facing burnout.

One thing I never heard mention of in college or even at the state or district level was a way to help ministers and their church staff at the *emotional* level. Working in ministry can weigh heavily on marriages, sometimes even destroying them. The things pastors hear, the attacks they face, the feelings of utter isolation, and the weight pastors carry, is unimaginable to those not in ministry.

I often say people walk into my office and "throw up all over my desk." What I mean by this is, there is a seeming never-ending stream of people recounting their painful stories to me. I hear these agonizing accounts every single week of ministry, but pastors usually don't get to vent even though we need to probably more than most.

There is a way to overcome this isolation, however, but this highly personal subject requires absolute transparency and integrity, and the right people to pull it off. The answer is a simple word that needs to be implemented, practiced, preached, and declared daily.

That word is *accountability*.

Don't think this book is only for pastors, though. Even though I have included a chapter just for pastors, anyone would benefit by reading *Simple Accountability.* The method I show is for any person struggling in their walk with Christ. This means those battling with specific sin, and those just trying to stay on the straight and narrow in a very difficult and crushing world. *Simple Accountability* is for anybody who wants to grow in the grace and knowledge of Christ. It will benefit anyone who dares to bravely confess their weaknesses and sins, those who want others to pray for them, and those who desire Godly council and wisdom for challenging situations. It is for all who desire to be successful and blessed in their lives. To be frank, though, it is truly for all of us because we all need accountability.

Simple Accountability is for anybody who wants to grow in the grace and knowledge of Christ.

In college I made some really good friends who were pursuing the same ministerial endeavors and we truly wanted to make a difference in the world where God would call us. We loved the Lord, we loved each other, and we loved the call that God had placed on our lives. Hearing the stories and experiences of seasoned pastors and missionaries during a class or chapel service was not enough, however, to understand the complexities of something we had never done before.

We were told we would be lonely in ministry, that we would face hard times in the work of ministry, but that there would be some joy in ministry, yet nobody ever said, "Find someone you can trust and tell them everything you are dealing with." Nobody told us to share with some trusted peer every temptation we would face, every frustration, and then remind them that they could do the same and we would listen.

The purpose of this book *is to say precisely that.*

I discovered long ago that I needed to talk to somebody; I needed men to bounce my ideas off, and share the frustrations I sometimes face. In the following chapters I will share my own stories of how those men have poured into my life both during trying times, as well as those times of great gain and victory.

Most important, I am going to lay out a method of accountability that has worked for me since Bible college. I cannot say it is the only way or the best way, it is just the way I do it and I figured it would help others as well. Every Sunday afternoon for almost thirty years now, I have called or sent an email to certain men with the particulars of my previous week. These conversations included details of my personal life, my marriage and family, and things pertaining to my church. I have sent them to men I trusted to pray for me and to encourage and advise me, but most important, to hold me accountable for the way I approach life and ministry. I have sent them to men on my board who will factually know if what I say about a service occurred, or if a need in the congregation is real. I try to tell them as much as I can about situations I face, because if I don't I am not being as authentically accountable to them as I need to be.

As a pastor, I am first of all very human. I realize I have been impacted by my childhood, my unique traumas, my circle of friends, my ministry endeavors, the everyday challenges of ministry, and the life-choices I have made along the way. Throw in a daily, personal life with a wife and three kids, what *they* are dealing with in life, and what it's like growing up in a minister's home, and you'll see just how human I am. Still, I know this works, so this contribution is my way to help men and women, teens, and even kids discover that accountability is a powerful and necessary habit to keep

Far too often, we hide behind our masks with our public lives being very different to our private lives.

us holy, right, and on the straight and narrow. I encourage you to get your heart ready for the journey because this needs to stick; it needs to last for a lifetime. My ultimate desire is what I have experienced will be a help to men especially, since we are held accountable by God as the heads of our homes, but I sincerely pray it helps anyone who decides to read it.

Far too often, we hide behind our masks with our public lives being very different to our private lives. We conceal our struggles and assume a false front. We pretend to be better, stronger, and more industrious than we are. I would not always call it a lie, although at times it is. It is simply that we like to be viewed favorably by our peers. We want to make a great impression at all times on everyone who sees us. We want to appear solid and stable, without blemish, and nearly perfect in all settings. Sadly however, we are not, and left unchecked, this can compound into significant problems. This is why we all need accountability.

Chapter One

What Is Accountability Anyway?

W ould you agree that to avoid the risk of misunderstandings it is always best to start with clear definitions of what is being discussed? When reading this book, it is especially important you know exactly what I mean when I convey something, so it would be good to begin with a dictionary definition of the word *accountable*.

The American Heritage Dictionary defines the word *accountable* as *answerable* and *responsible*.[1] That gives us some insight into the word but to understand what it means to be answerable and responsible we also need to investigate the root word *account*. According to the same source, an account means *a description of events; narrative, a set of reasons; explanation, a record of statement; business dealing; money received or spent, and to consider or regard (for actions)*[2] (parentheses mine). In other words, the first definition means a record of events according to *you*, and the second definition means a documented record of business dealings, which is far more objective than the former. In both cases, the bottom line is a *clarifying lifestyle*. What do I mean?

Whether you are a bookkeeper tracking income and expenses for a church or business, a manager of a large firm or business, proceeding through the self-checkout at a store, or approaching a traffic light turning red, you are answerable and responsible for your actions. Your record of your daily life events needs to be honest to yourself (and God), and your actions should withstand an objective scrutiny by others. In other words, you are to be answerable to yourself, God, and others, which means taking responsibility for your actions. Accountability should be part of your everyday real life.

We must also realize words can have different meanings on the street or in the office, in the context of conversation, and even just in passing. Words may have counters or opposites, like good and evil, big and small. Webster's Collegiate Thesaurus tells us the word *account* has synonyms meaning *use, worth, regard,* and *explanation.*[3] These are other words that shine more light on the usage and the meaning of the word. The same thesaurus tells us the antonym (opposite meaning) for accountable is *unaccountable.*[4] In other words, unaccountable means we do not tell the whole story, we do not give an adequate explanation, and are not taking full responsibility or being inaccurate in our accounting. Unfortunately, that characterizes far too many of us, both in the church and out.

At this point I need to get personal: I am a Christian, a husband, a father, a pastor, and a student. In all of those areas, and every other area of my life, I am required by God to be accountable. After all, 1 Peter 1:15-16 (NASB) says "But like the Holy One who called you, be holy yourselves also in all your behavior; because it is written, 'YOU SHALL BE HOLY, FOR I AM HOLY'". You see, there is truly no excuse for our wrong behavior or our lousy attitudes. We have the Holy Spirit to help us if we are genuinely seeking to live in obedience to God. If we conduct ourselves in an unacceptable manner, publicly or privately, God is not glorified. When I hear someone talk about the "hypocrites in the church," I realize that the people referring to the hypocrites needed to familiarize themselves with that verse. Whether accurate or not, this accusation does, however, reveal that Christians are accountable for how they live. Others should have no doubt we are

Christians and the fruit of our lives should be evidence of that fact.

These verses from 1 Peter have resonated with me since my first years at college where I was surrounded by many different kinds of Christians. I came from Jasonville, Indiana—a small rural community in Greene County. The population of our town was about 1,500 at the time, with a small school system, one stoplight, several churches (it was a great place to be born and raised). Then I attended Central Bible College—an Assemblies of God college in Springfield, Missouri. Springfield was a bigger city with a population of 141,000 people, and provided bigger opportunities. The college boasted international students from around the world, and students and pastors' kids from across the nation. I knew students who were kicked out for numerous reasons during the four years I was there, I knew pompous students from bigger churches who looked down on others from smaller churches or communities, and I knew struggling students with depression and fears about not making it in ministry. Out of this widely varied group, I ultimately met and made friends with people who truly wanted to live right and make a difference with their lives and ministry.

It was those specific friends on the ground floor of Flower Dorm (we called it "The Foundation") who sparked my interest in accountability. Our group started praying together and doing Bible studies on Wednesday nights. We prayed in the prayer room on that floor, and started sharing our needs and our fears. We shared our pains from the past as well as our current struggles. This was a life changing experience for me because these guys didn't judge, and they didn't talk to others about what we shared or struggled

"Iron sharpens iron, so one man sharpens another."

with in those times together. It was absolutely liberating to know that someone else was also praying about my personal struggles. Being human however, even attending a Bible college surrounded by great preaching, teaching, and friends, it still meant I had faults and a great need for accountability.

This brings us to another Bible verse which I see as a depiction of accountability, "Iron sharpens iron, so one man sharpens another"

(Proverbs 27:17, NASB). If you have ever lifted weights, you understand the value of a spotter. This is the individual who stands behind the bar as you lift so that if you get into trouble, and you're unable to lift the weights to the support guard, he grabs the bar and helps you get it up to safety. Make no mistake, the spotter can literally save your life by keeping the heavy bar from crushing your ribs, neck, or worse. The lifter not only depends on the spotter to help him accomplish the lift and to do it safely, but this also enables the lifter to push his limits and increase his strength.

The literal translation of the verse is "Iron by iron is sharpened, And a man sharpens the face of his friend" (YLT), with the word "face" referring to the personality or character of the individual. To say it another way, the interaction of accountability between friends will make them sharp as a razor. Each person becomes a shaping tool for the other. There is always room for someone to criticize a spiritual man because a spiritual man realizes the constructive aspect of it. It does not mean we have to accept all criticism, but it does mean we listen to those who have proven themselves to authentically watch and invest in our lives. When we are accountable to others like this, their advice will mostly be wisdom and direction we need to hear.

If you have ever sharpened a knife, you probably did so because it was dull and practically useless for the task at hand. You can still use a dull knife, but its effectiveness will be greatly diminished. Many also understand that the wisdom of youth (or lack thereof) is mostly not ready for prime-time. Neuroscientists say that the human brain doesn't fully develop until our late 20's and even into our early 30's.[5] The author of the article even suggests we are on a trajectory in life and maturity. What this says to me is there are patterns we need to develop early in life that help us make wise decisions for our futures. Accountability is one of the surest ways I know to develop such patterns. To say it again, we need accountability and transparency in every area of our lives to be successful and Christ-like, and from this evidence we need to start as soon as possible.

Solomon, who was recognized as the wisest man who has ever lived said, "Remember also your Creator in the days of your youth"

(Ecclesiastes 12:1a, NASB). He likewise said,

⁹ Two are better than one because they have a good return for their labor. ¹⁰ For if either of them falls, the one will lift up his companion. But woe to the one who falls when there is not another to lift him up. Ecclesiastes 4:9-10 (NASB)

Solomon teaches that it's good to have a friend around to pick you up when you fall, and he points out that two are better than one because of the increased return on their labor. What he means is two people working together toward a common goal will be able to accomplish that goal quicker and more effectively. The benefit is exponential instead of doubled.

Solomon also talks about the righteous saying, "For a righteous man falls seven times, and rises again" (Proverbs 24.16a, NASB). Since he references the two laboring together and helping the other to get up when he falls, we see a repeated idea and a suggestion. The suggestion is that the righteous man has friends who keep him accountable, and help him when he is weak or stumbling. Solomon, the wise king, made it clear that someone walking with us in our journey is not just a good idea, but a necessary requirement for life.

We need someone to walk beside us who will care about how we live, how we talk, and how we treat others. We need someone who will make sure we continue in the faith and stay on the straight and narrow, but we especially need someone who will care about our soul—that inner part of who and what we are in an eternal sense. Understand that this means accountability is far more than someone looking over your shoulder; *it is someone engaged in cultivating your life.* You need others invested in you, and you need to invest in others.

Accountability is far more than someone looking over your shoulder; it is someone engaged in cultivating your life.

I discovered how critical this is after one year of full-time ministry when I went through an extremely difficult situation as a youth pastor in my home church. A key relationship in my life had literally exploded and left me blind and deaf to the world around me. I became a diabetic through the stress and strain of that situation, and I felt like my life was literally unraveling at the seams. I had lost fifty pounds in four weeks and ended up in the hospital with a 1,742 glucose level. All that happened after running my twenty-first marathon and being in the best shape of my life. I was a pastor so I felt limited in what I could say to anybody about my suffering. You see, pastors are supposed to have it all together, but I was confused and scared. I needed to vent and needed to do it sooner than later.

At 2:00 a.m. on a Monday morning, after a Sunday of feeling very alone and isolated, laying on a picnic table at a local state park, I sulked. I was never suicidal, but I was depressed and weary from having no answers to my situation and no friends I could truly talk to, or even admit anything to. That is when a friend's face from The Flower Dorm flashed through my mind and I decided to call him the next day. He lived several states and a time zone away, and there would be no such thing as email for a few years, but I needed to talk to him. I found his number through directory assistance and called the next day, rekindling a friendship that I desperately needed. I drove out to see him and spent a few days at his house. That is when it started.

I made a call every week to share what I was going through in my personal life. I never held back with the temptations I faced, the emotional struggles I endured, or the loneliness I suffered. Then something remarkable happened. As my friend prayed for me he began to share his pains too: his marital issues, and his challenges at church. So I prayed for him in return. Over time we both grew, we made spiritual gains, and we both got better. I know I got better because I got it all out, and because someone stood with me in my battles. I was better and my friend was better because of the accountability we had in and with one another. Iron was sharpening iron and it was changing my life.

Now, over twenty-five years later, I want to share how it works so I can help as many other people as I can. This is because all of us need someone to hold us accountable before God and others. Again, I'm not saying it is "THE" model, just "a" model that has helped me, and I pray it helps you as well. It worked then and it works for me today, so if you aren't doing any sort of accountability, maybe you should start here. I have had over thirty separate accountability partners at different times over the last twenty-eight years. A few have been there for the long haul, while a few hung in for only a few months as they realized they were not able to share as deeply as they needed to.

Don't be fooled—it is not easy to do and not for those with secrets they are committed to keeping to themselves. Genuine accountability requires sheer intestinal fortitude because you have to be as transparent as you possibly can. That scares everybody who starts the process, but it does get easier. Even for men.

Men typically don't like to share their weaknesses or their problems. It is an inerrant part of our sinful nature and our rebellion against anybody discovering our innermost weaknesses and darkness. We don't want to perceive any man gaining an advantage over us, or seeing our true weaknesses, so we stay quiet and refuse to declare our sins, our secrets, and even our temptations to anybody for any reason. Yet James 5:16 says to confess our sins to one another. That can stop us in our tracks because our sins are personal and reserved for our memory and our minds only. The hard

The power of sin is in secrecy—our secrecy; and that secrecy is killing our walk with the Lord.

truth is we don't want anyone to know who we really are. We want no one to know our darkest secrets or the temptations we can't overcome. No one asks, and we don't tell. The power of sin is in secrecy—our secrecy; and that secrecy is killing our walk with the Lord.

Let's go back to the scripture in James. What is your reaction to James writing those words describing your need to confess your sins? Are you bothered by it or offended by the idea of someone knowing your sins and your habits? In all reality, when is the last time you told your deepest darkest secret to anybody? To your wife or husband? To your best friend or college buddy? To your pastor? Have you ever really lived this verse out at any given time in your life? I imagine the answer is likely no but this probably includes most of humanity; those who have lived, are living now, and those who will follow the pattern of life in the future.

Thankfully, the Bible is not silent about accountability. As we have already covered, the definition of accountability is very simple, it is basically "an obligation or willingness to accept responsibility or to account for one's actions." Some additional synonyms associated with accountability are *answerability*, *culpability*, and *burden*. These words have an almost legal sense to them as they imply burden of proof rests on the person responsible for the behavior, activity, or choices made. Consider the questions above and think about how often we fail in our Christian walk. How often do you beat yourself up for failing again at the same sin, for letting words slip, or having an attitude that comes out unexpectedly? For the most part, we hide what we really are from everybody around us.

One other point I need to make early on is that accountability provides an excellent opportunity for confrontation with purpose. It allows those we trust with our secrets and weaknesses to address our condition. It permits penetrating questioning on their part because we have invited them to evaluate our life. When we trust someone with our darkest secrets and wild imaginations we are asking them to advise us and counsel us and sharpen us. We are asking someone else to fight beside us and for us. We are asking a friend to walk with us and to help us keep a level head when the enemy attacks and assaults.

We are asking for help, plain and simple.

Remember where we started in this chapter? Accountability is not a temporary situation. A journey is traveled from one location to another and so is this life, whether you believe there is something on the other side of it or not. We will all find out one day, but as a Christian who believes in Heaven, I will take as much help to get there as I can. I am thankful for those who have been my accountability partners over the last three decades of my life. They have accepted me and have also chiseled away my rough edges, and I let them. Yes it was painful at times and embarrassing at others. There were occasions I even resisted, because from time to time I did not like what I saw of my real self in the mirror of my friend's account. Still, I am so glad they kept me accountable and made me push through it because I became better every time.

The way I am going to lay out my method in this book is very simple: first of all, I will explain why we need accountability. Second, I will advise you on how to pray the right people in to help you on the journey, how to pick a partner, and how close you should be to them at the start. Third, I will give you an idea on what a starting point in an accountability relationship looks like. Fourth, I will guide you on how to stay connected for the long haul. Finally, I will bring some resources to the table to help you in the journey. These are personal insights I have gained from doing this for almost thirty years at the time of this writing.

Let's get started.

Chapter Two

Why We Need Accountability

As a college student in Southern Missouri there were plenty of cave systems to explore in my spare time. Many a weekend encompassed gathering old clothes, covering the car seats with trash bags, loading up with headband lights, flashlights, extra batteries, then entering a deep, dark cave with friends. We would encounter bats, both hibernating and sometimes stirred up, which always made for rather colorful conversations about what would happen if one of us contracted rabies. We'd pass water-filled low spots, stalactites and stalagmites, frogs and lizards, and thick cave mud. When several of us spent a night in one of those caves, I discovered what darkness truly was. Since there is zero ambient light, your eyes never get used to the darkness, you lose track of time, and your internal sense of direction is affected for the duration of your stay. These are things you simply cannot predict unless you've experienced them, or have been told about them. When the lights go out, the darkness invades, engulfing you to the point of seeming suffocation. Some of those with us could not stand it and had to leave. Those who stayed had to guard their wits and intentionally remain calm.

A Dark Darker Than the Darkest Dark

I remember a professor explaining that one of the Greek words for dark could be translated as "a dark that is darker than the darkest dark." I have never forgotten that definition nor how disturbing the concept was to me then. The truth is I still find it disturbing to this day. In his letter to the Ephesians Paul speaks of this darkness:

> [12] For our struggle is not against flesh and blood, but against the rulers, against the powers, against the world forces of this darkness, against the spiritual *forces* of wickedness in the heavenly *places*. Ephesians 6:12 (NASB)

This deep darkness is the enemy Paul describes as stalking us, attacking us, harassing us, ever trying to immobilize us. Who wants to fight that kind of enemy alone? There are forces hiding in the shadows who want to surprise and attack us, and that darkness fuels and feeds them. Sadly, history makes it obvious that this enemy is also very effective.

Jesus said "The thief comes only to steal and kill and destroy; I came that they may have life, and have it abundantly" (John 10:10, NASB). There is an enemy—a hateful and spiteful enemy—that is deliberately focused on destroying your spiritual walk with the Lord. He is not out to merely make you miserable or give you a sinus headache, he is not simply trying to frustrate you in traffic, or test your patience in the retail checkout counter–make no mistake that Satan's goal is to destroy you, your marriage, your children, your reputation, and your integrity. What is his primary strategy to accomplish that? Keeping you unaccountable and disconnected is his best way to ensure you will never grow in the grace and knowledge of Christ. Unguarded by others, unchecked by friends, and unwatched by those close to you will leave you desolate and empty, setting you up as a prime target for the darkness that seeks to engulf you.

In 1 Peter 3:18 Peter encourages us to grow in the grace and knowledge of Christ. The knowledge part comes from the Word of God itself, but the grace part is found in your day-to-day life. Grace is a rubber-meets-the-road idea to help you in real life, where it happens, and when it happens. It is found in the joy of welcoming a child into this world, yet it is also the flat tire at 2:00 a.m., and it's the bad news the doctor just told you or someone you love. Life happens whether we like it or not. Challenges erupt almost daily in our lives, and every day we face various temptations. It may be lust or pride, or perhaps an attitude that is way out of line for a believer. Every day there is an enemy attacking our holiness and our character, and most of the time we forget about this spiritual warfare.

Peter also reminds us that we need to "be diligent to be found by Him (Christ) in peace, spotless and blameless," (parentheses mine—2 Peter 3:14, NASB). In other words, we must not only be ready for the return of Jesus, but we must be *living ready* while we are watching for His return. We should be evaluating our lives daily, checking our thoughts, and even asking others to inspect our fruit.

Jesus gave the world and the church the right to judge us when He stated, "You will know them by their fruits" (Matthew 7:16, NASB). The context of this verse deals with false prophets, but the principle that our lives bear fruit can't be easily dismissed. As we grow, learn, and mature, our decisions and lifestyle leave opportunity for others to judge what we produce. Others have the right to condemn or qualify who we are and what we are. The judging aspect of life gets taken out of context too often, because we

We must not only be ready for the return of Jesus, but we must be living ready *while we are watching for His return.*

forget that we judge others through the lens and frame of our own successes and failures. Our life is the testimony of how we live and Who we live for, so to suggest that others cannot address what we are in public is counter-productive to growth. Assessment by others is good for us and necessary. If you have ever gone through an employee evaluation you will understand that the supervisor is informing you where your work is excellent and also where you need to improve. It is nothing more than accountability reflecting on what is seen by others.

The War for the Mind

I would love to sit down with the apostle Paul some day and get a sense of his demeanor. I see him as a no-nonsense kind of guy who never backed down from doing anything he knew was right, or was God's will. He was zealously stubborn for righteousness after realizing the righteousness he formerly pursued was empty and shallow. He also had friends like Luke the physician, the younger men Timothy and Titus, and Barnabas with whom he fell into an argument which separated them for several years. I see Paul's strength in his mindset. He knew what he believed and he knew why he believed it. He was settled in it, and he understood the nature of the war for his mind.

Paul explained it in the following way:

> [3] For though we walk in the flesh, we do not war according to the flesh, [4] for the weapons of our warfare are not of the flesh, but divinely powerful for the destruction of fortresses. [5] *We are* destroying speculations and every lofty thing raised up against the knowledge of God, and *we are* taking every thought captive to the obedience of Christ, [6] and we are ready to punish all disobedience, whenever your obedience is complete. 2 Corinthians 10:3-6 (NASB)

Paul makes it clear in this passage that the fight for solid faith is in the battlefield of the mind. Our thought life influences our physical life. When Jesus equated lust with a physical sexual act in Matthew 5:28 He was making it clear that our thoughts have consequences. The Sermon on the Mount was spoken both to a Jewish and a foreign crowd, but the moral values Jesus preached were understood by every culture. The Roman soldier, the widow, the kids, the young man determining his next steps—they all heard very different counsel than the advice they were used to receiving.

The fight for solid faith is in the battlefield of the mind.

Jesus reminded the people they were responsible for their actions and their thoughts. He reminded them that their public life reflected on their faith, because the salt of the Earth and the light of the world idea carried a notable responsibility on their part. Paul's statement that "we are ambassadors for Christ" (2 Corinthians 5:20, NASB) means we represent Jesus in all walks of life. We are His representatives to the watching world. Jesus' words in Matthew 7 spell out the need for accountability even further because of the multitude of opposing choices we face. Jesus described two ways of life (7:13-14), two kinds of teaching represented by two kinds of trees (7:15-20), two ways to approach the Kingdom (7:21-23), and two kinds of builders (7:24-27). We make choices every day that determine our successes and our failures. We can do it our way or God's way, we can plant the tree next to good resources or plant it in cement. There is only have one way into the Kingdom, but can try to make our own way by building on a shaky foundation and ignoring the True way.

Many of our choices are made without any solid thought behind them, and we sometimes flippantly go down a road we never should have. I will share some interesting stories from my childhood and youth over the course of the book, but when I was a kid, I spent a lot of time outside in the woods behind my house with friends from the area. We always carried rifles and shotguns, and had plenty of ammunition, fireworks, and coolers full of glass bottle pop. We had an assortment of food, tents, and bicycle trails to ride on. We swam unguarded in water-filled pits left over from strip mining, and had diving and cannonball competitions off a thirty-foot cliff that stretched out over those pits. We climbed around on abandoned mining equipment and discovered various mine entrances over the years. We spent countless nights around a fire, sleeping in a tent or on the ground. Believe it or not, our parents never worried about any of us. My mom would have a heart attack if she knew half the things we did back then, but we were relatively safe, and I am still breathing today.

It was the seventies, and the things I mentioned all happened before I was ten. Some of the guys were older so they watched out for the younger ones, and there was always someone with a sense of responsibility around at all times. It was assumed that someone would jump in to save anyone who was drowning, or make sure that when we were shooting bottles we understood gun safety. There were no cell phones and no internet, so we enjoyed our time outside and lived life as full as a bunch of kids could.

As we got older, the bike trails grew over from non-use, the tents rotted in our garages, those bikes became cars, and we got jobs. We grew up and out of the childish beginnings of our journey. As friends we drifted off to different places and even different stages—military, college, marriage, and other phases of life. I still miss the camaraderie of those days, the stunts we pulled and the bonds we made, but later I recognize a common feature that kept us safe during those times— someone was always watching us, and that was important.

Family watched out for the kids, and neighbors watched those same kids from their windows. When we were back in the woods and it was time to come home my mom would ring a huge bell she had in front of our house. You could hear it at least three miles away, and when my brother and I heard it we knew it meant to be home in the next thirty minutes. It was her way of keeping us safe and calling us home to eat or to clean up and get to bed. She was keeping us accountable and being a responsible mother at the same time. She trusted us out in the woods because she knew who would be there with us and she knew their parents. She knew we were close by, but because "boys will be boys", I am sure she still worried. I grew up with people watching out for me, and I learned to do the same for others.

Never Go It Alone

My brother, Darin, became a diabetic at the age of nine. This complicated his life as well as our family life at first as we tried to understand exactly how the disease worked. He and I played little league baseball together so I monitored his condition on the field. If we were back in the woods I made sure the cooler had juice and candy in case he had a low blood-sugar episode. On the ball field I began to recognize the signs of a glucose drop. Even at school I would be asked by the nurse or the school secretary (who was my aunt) if he was alright. We were always close, and the illness gave me a greater reason to watch and observe his life. We fought like brothers would fight, and we got along well enough to have a lot of fun when we were younger. There is one winter event though, that stands out with just how badly we needed each other and needed to have somebody watching out for us.

During the seventies my father had a hardware store in Terre Haute, Indiana. Along with the hardware, he also sold other items like toys, carpet, and tile, but my favorite item he sold was fireworks. He had access to some of the more professional and commercial fireworks, which simply meant bigger, brighter, and more dangerous. Every Fourth of July he would set off a show in our yard that would draw large crowds of people. My father would list the order in which he wanted the fireworks brought to him, and my brother and I shared that responsibility. As a reward for that job he would give us a box full of larger bottle rockets. By larger, I mean the rockets that were three feet in length and had a head of at least eight inches long. These were premium rockets as they had a large explosive capability. More significant is that we discovered they were waterproof.

One winter, Darin and I went down to the ice-covered pond behind our house and cut a hole with a shovel at the edge of the pond to do some ice fishing. I am not sure which one of us thought of it, but the idea was "I wonder if those rockets would produce a cool light show under the ice or just go very far and break?" I walked back home to the garage, grabbed three of them and returned to test our theory. I stood on the edge of the pond, lit the big rocket, then held it under the water right before it launched, aiming it straight out. Well the rocket shot about twenty-five feet out from the shore, exploded, and cracked the ice with a huge bright and colorful blast of fire. We were ecstatic! It was so wonderful that we spent the next two hours blowing that pond's ice-cover to smithereens. No one was hurt, except for nearly-frostbitten hands from holding those rockets under the water. Then another idea hit us. The next time the ice was thick enough, we should go out and launch the rockets from the middle of the pond, and maybe even stand above where the rocket would explode. A fourth grade education in science had taught us nothing about the fragility of ice on a fifty-foot deep pond so we decided it was a relatively good idea.

When I was ten years old, it was the year after a major blizzard in the Seventies and it had been brutally cold. We checked the ice, we walked it, we kicked it, we even drilled it, and were happy to find about eight to ten inches of ice. We spent the next hour drilling enough holes to make a big enough opening to get the rockets down into the water under the ice. Then we started lighting and aiming rockets with a frenzied speed. Two of our neighbor friends were watching us from the shore because they did not believe the rockets would stay lit or explode underwater. Once they realized it worked, they raced out onto the ice with us. After about four or five launches in different directions I said I wanted to see one blow up under my feet. I walked about thirty feet away and Darin lit one, held it under the water, and aimed it my way. It blew up about five feet in front of me in spectacular fashion. Then everyone there wanted to see a rocket explode under their feet as well.

There is a reason common sense keeps a lot of people alive, and the four people in the middle of that pond were about to find that out, and just how much they needed each other. With about fifteen rockets already exploded under the pond's surface, we were about to understand the need for accountability, and most of all, common sense. Darin had walked closer to the edge of the pond because the ice was getting cracked in the middle areas, so from the side of the pond, I lit one of our last rockets and watched it streak toward him. What I remember is not the colors coming through the ice as the rocket exploded, but my brother falling through the ice.

Instantly the other two guys and I ran over to that edge of the pond but we could not see Darin anywhere in the water. The water was about seven or eight feet deep and one of the guys immediately went in to find Darin. I had on a parka and boots, but I also jumped in to do what I could. I immediately realized two things: the water was deathly cold and I was being dragged down by my heavy clothes. As I struggled frantically, I thought about my brother, my two friends, and if I was going to live to see another day. Suddenly, a hand jerked the back of the parka, pulled me out of the water and dragged me onto the ice. I lay on the frozen lake coughing and spitting up water beside my brother who was doing the same thing. The brothers then lifted us up and helped us walk to their house less than a quarter of a mile away.

While we warmed up in front of a big kettle fire barrel in a reloading shed we quietly but excitedly reflected on what could have happened.

We also never told my mother, and although we still blew rockets up under the ice over the next several years, we never stood on the ice over the explosion ever again. We had learned a big lesson there, and not just about rockets and ice. The lesson was to *never go it alone*. The lesson was to have observers in everything you do, because it might just save your life. You see, two are better than one because when one falls in the ice-cold pond in January there is somebody there to drag you out to safety.

It's funny how the most important lessons are often learned the proverbial hard way. I became interested in lifeguarding shortly after that event and later pursued it. I am sure the reason was because somebody had been there and had watched me sink. They had also prevented my brother and me from drowning. We always need somebody watching out for us, and we need to be accountable to others for it to work.

Two Are Better Than One

I recently jumped out of a relatively good airplane while tandem-strapped to a guy from New Zealand. At 14,000 feet, I was glad the guy helping me experience skydiving for the first time had done it before. In the over 10,000 jumps he had done, many had been with somebody like me attached to him. He had started the same way, strapped to somebody else for his first skydiving jump. He enjoyed it so much he decided to make it a career and now helps people see the world from a breathtaking new view. We all start at the same place, we all experience that first time of doing something, but we can always learn how to sharpen that thing we do. Having someone beside us to advise, to steer, to rebuke even, makes a difference in where we are going, and to our condition when we arrive.

Another point to make here is that accountability is not to just keep us out of trouble. Coach, trainer, and mentor are all words that could be used to describe an accountability partner—they advise and counsel you in your walk, steering you through critical decisions. These roles are very much like a guidance counselor in a high school setting—the guidance counselor's job is to guide incoming freshmen to select the right classes as they head for graduation. On the other end of the spectrum, they guide seniors through the college application and financial aid part of it. They walk with the student from the start of high school to completion and help prepare them for college. Four years of investment in each student is the price, but what matters most for results is that the student listen and follow the advice for those four years.

God designed us to need each other. In Genesis 3:18 God stated that it was not good for man to be alone, so God made a suitable mate for him. Since the context of Solomon's statements about two being better than one are not about marriage, it makes sense that God put friendships into play because we all need somebody to help guide us. We have parents, teachers, and leaders, but we still need the friend who

God designed us to need each other.

sticks closer than a brother (Proverbs 18:24). When Solomon wrote that, he implied the need for deep lifetime relationships. I need people to be honest with me when I am not being honest with myself. I need people to see the holes in my logic. I need people who will catch me when I say something with an edge, and remind me that I should have not said it. I need someone to pour into my life and make me more valuable as a human being than I am right now.

Whether on ice or firm ground, you can never tell when an unexpected or unlikely event will occur, and these "freak accidents" happen all the time. News articles appear often about how someone died because something unimaginable happened, because life itself is unpredictable. I have performed funerals for people in every decade of life, including a stillborn baby. I knew one man in his nineties—a friend of my father—who had lived as rough a life as you can imagine. He was an alcoholic, had been a cigar smoker since he was twelve, had a multitude of scars from his work, as well as fights, and lived without any fear of God. He told me he wanted me to do his funeral but had some demands: he said he had lived hard all of his life, had been successful, and was a self-made man, so he wanted no credit given to God for his longevity in any funeral message I might give.

Over the next several years, I witnessed the man go through severe physical agony as lung cancer engulfed his life. His family was divided since his twelve children were from five marriages. Most of his kids loathed him because he only rewarded success, and most of them had not measured up anywhere near his standards. He never trusted banks and was just a staunchly grim individual. Bitter probably best describes him. His third wife, the only one who still came by to see him, called and asked me to visit him in the nursing home several weeks before he died. He was an expired man for sure, and he confessed how lonely he had been his entire life. People hated to work for him because he was a hard taskmaster, paid as little as he possibly could, and yelled at everybody. He was mean-spirited to the core and blamed his dad for everything he had become.

Upon arrival, I asked if he knew why I was there. That I was a youth pastor fresh from Bible College with little experience in deathbed conversions did not matter as he started crying to the point of sobbing. After about ten minutes of gut-wrenching tears, he gained control of himself and told me he was afraid to die. He admitted his life had been a mess, his kids hated him, he had mistreated every one of his wives, and had cheated his employees for decades. He confessed all his sins, deceit, and back room deals. He was thoroughly broken. He made it clear that he had never told anyone the things he had just shared with me, yet he still felt burdened and without peace. I reminded him that although he was on borrowed time he could still remedy some of the issues with his family.

The man had not been to church since he was a child, and had not spoken to several of his kids in over twenty years. He had been a harsh man, but at the point of death felt a great need to spill his history. I shared scripture with him and made the case for salvation. After a long while of listening, he asked if saying that prayer would fix him. I explained saying the prayer was just the beginning. He then asked me to lead him in the salvation prayer so I did, and when I opened my eyes he had the most profound tear-filled yet peaceful look on his face. He immediately requested that I ask his kids to come see him. I spoke to his third wife about this and she left to find several of them. Over the next three days he met with each of his kids, apologized, and begged for their forgiveness. He did the same with two of his former wives, although the other two refused to come to see him.

On the fourth day he died. At the end of his life he needed to share the weight of his soul, and he needed a physical human being to speak to. It did not make up for all the mistakes he had made with his family, friends or employees, and it didn't fix everything on this side of his life, but it brought relief to his soul. He felt the need to unload the burden of his soul and tell the awful truth about himself.

In other words, he desperately needed to be held accountable.

He needed to be accountable for his actions and for his life, and the only way to do this was to confess it from all the way back when it started. This is why you need to start being accountable now. If you wait too long it will be one long regretful confession with a wake of buried pain, shattered relationships, missed events, and apologies you never made along the way.

I hope I have adequately conveyed the importance of having someone who will hold you accountable in your life, and if so, you are probably wondering who you could select as your accountability partner. Picking your accountability partner(s) is going to be one of the most important decisions you make in your lifetime. Take your time and do it right. The next two chapters serve as my advice on just how you might do that.

Chapter Three

The Kind of People You Need

In keeping with our aim for clarity, I want to examine the meaning of the word "friend." The American Heritage Dictionary defines the word "friend" as "a person whom one knows, likes, and trusts."[6] In our younger years, these friends might be the kids we meet in kindergarten and those we play little league ball with. They are the neighborhood kids who ride the bus with us, and the ones with whom we shared stories and jokes. They are usually the people who are around the same age as us and who share our life experiences. We can recall all their idiosyncrasies and pet peeves, our shared events, our mutual laughter and tears. Growing up together, we learned many of the same things at the same times. We endured heartache and bruises together, along with bicycle wrecks that sometimes could have killed us. For me, the most important aspect of having friends is the accumulation of valuable moments as we mature—the shared experiences and the lessons learned.

As significant and treasured as your childhood friends are, I believe the friends you make in college have an edge over the friends you grew up with. It might be just my experience, but I really believe that. You may have grown up on the same street and played ball together, but did you share career goals? Did you pursue the same majors in college? Our interests and goals change and develop as we get older. You are a different person at twenty-two than you were at eighteen, and your life experience differs vastly even between those young ages. You might still have those friends from childhood, but the maturity and value of those relationships differ. Some of the closest friends I have today are the friends I made in college. This is because we shared similar career goals so we attended many of the same classes, ran in the same circles, gathered around the same professors, and followed similar paths in ministry.

Our environment also expands as we grow. Most colleges and universities are situated in metropolitan-type communities and unless you attended a large school system or lived in a larger community to begin with, the college experience was world-changing to you. The student population of a college is typically larger than that of the high school you attended, and the city in which the college is located is usually larger than the town in which you were born and raised. I say this as someone who grew up in a rural town thirty minutes from the largest community in our area. Where I live now—Burkesville, Kentucky—it requires at least a thirty-minute drive to the closest Wal-Mart, but I prefer to live in a community of this size; to raise my children safely and peacefully here. The point is that as we grow older our world gets bigger and the importance and value of friendships grows exponentially.

This has been true throughout the ages, and the Bible is filled with examples of strong relationships and close friendships. In the first part of Exodus 33:11 (NASB) we read, "Thus the Lord used to speak to Moses face to face, just as a man speaks to his friend." The implication in this verse is that friends speak to each other closely—they share their hearts, they laugh with one another, and they share difficult experiences. It is important to realize that under God's new covenant, He speaks to us at the friend level as well, and we know He will always be honest with us. *This,* I believe, is the real principle here; God wants to invest in us as our friend, to lead and guide us so we develop and mature on our journey. We develop our friendship with God by spending time with Him, and tuning in with our spirit to receive direction through our devotional life, through reading His Word, and through our prayer life–listening as well as speaking. Likewise, the fellowship we share in a church setting plays a huge part in receiving the discipleship we need for our spiritual walk.

Catch the Wind

As a kid, my brother and I did a lot of silly play-activities together, usually by my lead as I was older. On one occasion, however, Darin led me into a moment of painful stupidity I should have figured out before I jumped into it. When I was around five years old, my Aunt Betty made me a Superman costume from scratch and I paraded around in it often. My brother was about a year younger than me at the time and we both watched George Reeves play the character on TV, so flying was a goal for both of us. My brother managed to convince me that because I was wearing the Superman costume, naturally I could fly, so we fetched a ladder and climbed the roof onto our front porch. It was the fall season so we piled up plenty of leaves to keep me from dying if, for some unlikely reason, I was not able to fly on the first try.

First I walked from the angled part of the house roof to the edge of the porch roof several times, flapping my cape each time. I wet my finger and held it in the air to determine the direction of the wind. Once distance and wind direction had been determined, my brother counted down with eager expectation and I ran towards the edge with gusto, but stopped short of the gravity-defying leap as I reached the edge. After several attempts my brother grew angry at my lack of courage and yelled, "Just catch the wind!" I'm still not sure where he had picked up that phrase but it centered me. I took aim at the neighbor's roof about a hundred yards away before running up and launching myself off the edge of the roof. I only missed by about ninety-eight yards. Unfortunately I also missed the pile of leaves we had gathered, landed flat on my stomach, and couldn't catch a decent breath for the next twenty minutes.

My brother scrambled down from the roof and assessed the situation as any four year old would. His determination was that I was dead, so he ran into the house screaming, "Dana's dead! Dana's dead!" This, of course, grabbed the immediate attention of our mother, who dashed outside in terror. She found me sitting on the ground picking leaves and dirt out of my mouth, holding my gut but not crying. I was still in shock I suppose. After assessing the situation and realizing I had only *almost* died, my mom began yelling at me for doing something so stupid.

My mom then stripped that Superman suit off of me and left me laying on the grass in my underwear and socks. She then went inside and promptly called my grandmother who lived across the street. My grandmother marched over and switched me right where I lay in the front yard as cars went by. Thankfully none of the neighbors were watching, but looking back, I was very blessed there were no broken bones, chipped teeth, a cracked skull, or worse.

Apart from the insight gained regarding my apparent lack of superpowers and ability to fly, the lesson I learned was never to take my brother's advice regarding aerodynamics. Most important though, I learned about the importance of selecting from those around you, who can give you good advice. This is only one example in my childhood where I wish I had listened to my own common sense. The reality is we need to bounce our ideas, our plans, and our goals, off others who can be trusted to keep us safe in the process. In other words, we each need people we trust who will keep us accountable for our plans and our actions.

> *We each need people we trust who will keep us accountable for our plans and our actions.*

Covenantal Friendship

I would like to lay a foundation for this concept by examining a friendship we find outlined in the Bible. David's musical skills had caught the attention of King Saul, who was known for his demonically-influenced temper. In 1 Samuel 16:14 we are told the Spirit of God had departed from Saul, making him a very difficult person to be around.

David was given the job of playing the lyre to calm the king, and he eventually even became Saul's armor bearer (1 Samuel 16:21-23). Verse 21 reveals a deeper clue to the closeness of the relationship when it tells us Saul loved David deeply. Here it should be noted that friendships are extremely fragile—they can grow in maturity or cause murder with jealousy and poisoned agendas. This is clearly illustrated in the account of David, Saul, and Jonathan. David killing Goliath in 1 Samuel 17 resulted in a meeting with Saul's son, Jonathan, who became knit to David in friendship.

> [1] Now it came about when he had finished speaking to Saul, that the soul of Jonathan was knit to the soul of David, and Jonathan loved him as himself. [2] Saul took him that day and did not let him return to his father's house. [3] Then Jonathan made a covenant with David because he loved him as himself. [4] Jonathan stripped himself of the robe that was on him and gave it to David, with his armor, including his sword and his bow and his belt. [5] So David went out wherever Saul sent him, and prospered; and Saul set him over the men of war. And it was pleasing in the sight of all the people and also in the sight of Saul's servants. 1 Samuel 18:1-5 (NASB)

This God-ordained camaraderie between David and Jonathan would develop over several years. David, however, began to enjoy great success on the battlefield, leading Saul to eventually succumb to bitter jealousy over David's success. Scripture explains it in the following way:

> [6] It happened as they were coming, when David returned from killing the Philistine, that the women came out of all the cities of Israel, singing and dancing, to meet King Saul, with tambourines, with joy and with musical instruments. [7] The women sang as they played, and said, "Saul has slain his thousands, And David his ten thousand's." [8] Then Saul became very angry, for this saying displeased him; and he said, "They have ascribed to David ten thousands, but to me they have ascribed thousands. Now what more can he have but the kingdom?" [9] Saul looked at David with suspicion from that day on. 1 Samuel 18:6-9 (NASB)

David's success created such envy in Saul that on two occasions Saul hurled his spear at David while he played for the king (1 Samuel 18:10-11). Since Saul's mind was poisoned with suspicion, all David's motives and agendas were questioned, absolutely destroying any trust. Yet while one relationship soured, another was set on a course of honesty and success.

David was removed from Saul's presence and placed over thousands of soldiers where he continued to have tremendous success. Israel and Judah supported and loved David dearly (1 Samuel 18:12-16). Saul became so demonically swayed, he eventually asked his son, Jonathan, and his leaders, to orchestrate David's death. Jonathan would do no such thing, due to this brotherly love for David, so he warned his friend, sparing his life (1 Samuel 19:1-2). Jonathan reminded his father of David's loyalty to the king, buying him the time to escape and go on the run. Saul continued to pursue David but Jonathan met with David to warn him of his father's intentions. At that meeting Jonathan took the opportunity to make a covenant with the house of David (1 Samuel 20:16). This becomes significant so we need to dig a bit here.

The house of David included all of David's future family, and the weight of this relationship was destined to become even deeper over time. When Jonathan realized his father would not change his mind about David or his intentions to kill him, Jonathan urged David to leave the area for his own safety.

> [41] And as soon as the boy had gone, David rose from beside the stone heap and fell on his face to the ground and bowed three times. And they kissed one another and wept with one another, David weeping the most. 42 Then Jonathan said to David, "Go in peace, because we have sworn both of us in the name of the Lord, saying, 'The Lord shall be between me and you, and between my offspring and your offspring, forever.'" And he rose and departed, and Jonathan went into the city. 1 Samuel 20:41-42 (ESV)

Both men knew their friendship was strong and intact but they wept knowing they would probably not see each other again. Even though Jonathan's father hated his best friend, it did not change Jonathan's heart towards David. Jonathan warned David and saved his life, and in doing so placed a distance between the two friends. Of the two of them David wept the most, because as future king he was deeply indebted to Jonathan. The house of David would continue long after he and David were gone, but Jonathan committed his future and the future of his children to this covenant arising from the relationship. By warning David of Saul's plot to kill him, Jonathan had jeopardized his relationship with his father, and even his own life.

Above all Jonathan was loyal. He was gifted with commitment in a time when a person's word mattered. He was a peacemaker and a life saver. Jonathan would later lose his life alongside his father and brothers on Mount Gilboa (1 Samuel 31), and I can guarantee he never forgot his friend David, nor the bond they shared. David never forgot Jonathan either, nor the covenant between them. Attesting to this, we read in 2 Samuel that Jonathan had a son named Mephibosheth who was only five years old when his father died. Upon hearing of Saul and Jonathan's death, the boy's nurse feared for his life and fled to safety with him. In their haste to escape, the boy fell and was crippled (2 Samuel 4:4). Mephibosheth lived in hiding for many years, believing David would kill him as a supposed heir of Saul's. We can assume David believed him to be dead. Some time later David remembered his friendship with Jonathan and felt the need to honor him, asking the court if there was anyone left in Saul's house he could honor, based on the kindness he had received from Jonathan. Ziba, a servant in Saul's house, told the king about Jonathan's crippled son and explained where David could find him (2 Samuel 9:1-5).

When Mephibosheth was brought to King David, he fell on his face in fear. In words fitting for the moment, David told Jonathan's son not to be afraid. Then he told Mephibosheth that he would restore to him all the land that belonged to Saul for the sake of his father, Jonathan. Granting him the status of one of the king's sons, David said Mephibosheth would always eat at the king's table. This was a particularly significant honor for this crippled young man. It was far more than just an honor though, it was a tribute to Jonathan who had befriended David and saved his life. The land Mephibosheth had been given would be taken care of by servants, and Jonathan's son would have entry to the kings house and eat at his table for the rest of his life (2 Samuel 9:13).

This is a remarkable picture of what accountability brings to a friendship. Based on the trust and commitment shared in their relationship, David took responsibility for his friend's son for life. The relationship between the two men developed into something deeper than a friendship, spanning at least two generations. David honored his promise to the point of extending that commitment to his friend's son who David did not know. David cared so much for his friend that taking care of Jonathan's son was a no-brainer. He would share stories and rekindle the memories, but most of all David would help the son understand things about his father that he had no way of knowing. David would invest into Jonathan's son that which he could no longer invest into the relationship with his deceased friend.

The story of David and Jonathan highlights the fact that we need friends who will invest in us out of their own moral fiber and experience. We need people who will share their stories, especially the experiences

We need friends who will invest in us out of their own moral fiber and experience.

endured in agony. We need them to share the hard times, the good times, and the worst times, because it helps us better understand them. We need to make this personal and singular to get the point across—"I" need friends who will speak honestly to me about change required in my life. "I" need mentors who will draw out and refine the gold and silver in my character and talents. "I" need friends who will talk to me firmly and take me to the woodshed when necessary. "I" need friends who will truly hold and keep me accountable for my actions and my words. We all know this, but we intentionally ignore it at times to save ourselves the pain of discovery or confession.

I hope that by now you have friends in mind who could help you grow. I also imagine you already know who would *not* be a good candidate for the position. Ask yourself these questions: what do you specifically need to be accountable for, and what are the primary sins you fight? How are things in your marriage and with your kids? What is your language like at work and at the gym? I have some ideas and suggestions, even some surveys to help prepare both you and the person you will be accountable to. Get ready to confess and be uncomfortable, but mostly get ready to be free to let your light shine before men. Consider people who will call you out on behavior that is not Christ like, find someone who will—in genuine love—not go easy on you. And this is very important, find someone who will share their secrets with *you* or the balance in the relationship will never be complete.

There is something else I recommend: I encourage you to have an older person as your mentor, someone who has a wider stream of experience in life, and to heed the wisdom gained from that experience. I also suggest accountability with someone around your own age; someone with similar experiences and who is facing the same kind of life challenges. In addition, I think it is important to have a younger person in which to invest yourself as a mentor. In this way you can then help the next generation understand the necessity of accountability and encourage them to pass it on. Having someone pour into your life from their wisdom, as well as someone sharing the same kind of experiences, and an individual to pour into from your own understanding, brings a balance to all aspects of your life.

Chapter Four

Identifying Your Specific
Needs in Accountability

There was a laundromat in my home town that was frequently used as an amusement park. My friends and I would go in to that laundromat to check on one specific thing—we wanted to see an "Out of Order" sign on a large dryer in the back because that meant that a heating element was broken and the fun could begin. If any of us saw that sign it meant find the others, grab pillows, and meet at the laundromat within the hour.

It was never the same group of kids, but we all knew there could be no responsible adult in the laundromat at that time. So we would play the arcade games in the corner, watching the clock, waiting for the place to be empty. If someone was waiting for their laundry, we would shift out and ride around town and keep checking back to see if cars had left. People would start loads and leave so we had the washer and dryer times down to a science. We also knew that most people did not use the facility on Mondays, so it was prime-time for us. After little league ball practice or bike rides in town, we would load up on pop and candy at the Rexall drug store and head to the laundromat. We were a well-oiled machine because we had to be.

After arriving, we had established rituals and important jobs to perform. This ensured the fun was uninterrupted by the yelling owner or other annoyed patrons. We called ourselves "The Spinners," even though we never knew exactly who had coined that phrase. It was very appropriate and here is why: the first team would pack pillows into the broken dryer, then one kid would climb in and adjust himself between the metal ribs of the interior. The next team would get as many of the laundry carts that were available and pack them near the dryer. One or two kids would stand in front of that dryer with a pop or comic books in hand, lean against it trying to look like we were supposed to be there. There was always one of us at the door watching for patron traffic and of course, the police (we had learned to park the bikes behind the place because fifteen bicycles in front of a laundromat at noon was a dead give-away for shenanigans). At this point the quarters went in, the door was closed, and the kid inside began their ride.

Someone to Open the Door

Now I have seen about all you can imagine when the dryer started spinning—some kids yelling how cool it was on their first ride, others screaming "Stop!" in a guttural, primal shriek, I've seen giant bruises on highly visible parts of the body, kids so dizzy they fell over when they got out, and every now and then there were those covered in their own vomit because they were allowed to spin too long (this usually led to a quick exit upon discovery). Thirty seconds in the dryer was respectable, but everybody wanted to see how long they could go, and try to set new records. I once lasted three minutes and forty seconds, but it took me fifty minutes to get off the floor afterwards. I also wrecked my bike at least twelve times on the way home, so I walked it the rest of the way.

It was an entertaining way to occupy time in a small town, but it also carried incredible risks. You had to trust the door opener was actually watching the time, because for first-timers thirty seconds was a lot after launch. Also, just because you opened the door didn't mean the dryer stopped immediately, or that the kid would be on the bottom of the basket when it stopped. It was the trickiest part of the ride and required others to genuinely watch out for you. It's funny to me that even at that age (second to fifth grades), we recognized the need for accountability. You had to know you could trust the person to open the door if you needed it to stop, especially if the heating element actually started warming up. Yes, we discovered it wasn't always the heating element that was out of order, so that made for some interesting first rides.

I cannot remember how much pain this ride cost me or the other elementary school participants, but my memories are packed with questions from my mom about bruises and cuts, and why her pillows went missing for several hours on occasion. It was fun and cheap though, and it made celebrities of some of us. My sister's boyfriend was who originally told me about the dryer. He'd outgrown it but he encouraged me to enjoy the ride while I was

We definitely knew the risks, just like we know the risks we take today.

little. So, I did, and so did my buddies and we loved every minute of it. We had a blast, but we could never have done it without each other. Even when the police or patrons caught and berated us, being kids, our excuse was that we didn't know how dangerous it was. We definitely knew, though, just like we know the risks we take today.

"The Spinners'" system of accountability was something we lived out. I suppose we did not really understand how badly we could have been hurt. At that age we couldn't calculate the risk of being spun untethered in a commercial dryer, twenty miles from the nearest hospital. We never questioned if the door could get stuck or whether the spin cycle might not stop, and we hadn't even given the electrical breakers a thought. We never listened to the older ladies who yelled at us, claiming we were trying to break our necks on purpose, even when they threatened to tell our grandmas. I do still wonder, though, if the static in those dryers ever impacted our brains in some harmful way. Therein lies the value of hindsight over precaution, even when some precaution is used.

I am very glad somebody opened the door when I needed a break from spinning in that dryer. There was no internal button to abort the ride because the dryer was never intended to spin kid-sized humans for fun. We had hijacked its intended function and used it selfishly in ways I am sure no dryer engineer had ever dreamed of. We never intentionally hurt people or placed an out of order sign on the wrong dryer with ill will but we were foolish because we were kids without much life experience. Even so, we understood our actions (or lack of action) could hurt someone badly. Even as kids we knew we needed to watch out for others—our little brothers or sisters, our younger friends, and each other. There was always somebody reminding us of this.

Which Areas Are You Weakest?

I would like you to take some time right now to seriously look at your life and your behavior. Are you single, married, divorced, widowed, or alone by choice? What are your major temptations and how do you fight them? Is your prayer and devotional life solid, semi-strong, or is it nonexistent? Are you extroverted or introverted and how do you handle dealing with people? Are you kind, angry, bitter, generous, selfless, or selfish? Are you financially over-extended, content with your money situation, or drowning week-to-week? How do you treat your wife and your children? What behaviors do they see at home? How do you treat the people you work with, or the slow driver in front of you when you are in a hurry? Who are you during the mundane day-to-day transactions with everybody within your circle of influence? The reality of life is this: we are complicated individuals with different environmental stimulations and temptations, and we sometimes need help with an exit strategy. You really need someone to open the dryer door so you don't spin too long.

One of the first things you must do in becoming accountable is to admit which areas in your life are the weakest. For most men, sexual temptation is high on the list. Forget about saying it doesn't happen because that is the way men are wired, or at least how our wiring was impacted after Adam's sin in the Garden. Once you recognize your own unconcealed humanity, you understand how much you need Jesus to steer your life, and upright friends to encourage you to stay on the path. When you are able to share the darkness that sometimes surrounds you, then you are ready to step into serious accountability.

36

Think about your specific struggles. Is lust one of them? Is pride? Do you have an angry heart leading to heated words and pronounced impatience with others? Do you ever go too far with jokes or comments, sometimes to the point of causing offense and hurt? Are you a habitually late person, or do cause your boss headaches because of your work ethic? Do you cheat on your taxes, your classwork, or your spouse? You must realize these are the things you need to confess and be ready to address when being accountable or the process won't work. You

When you are able to share the darkness that sometimes surrounds you, then you are ready to step into serious accountability.

need to be able to share the good, the bad, and the ugly in you. It might seem impossible at first, but your comfort level and ability to be completely honest gets easier over time. Accountability *can* be accomplished if you stay on the path.

I find it interesting that in the book of James we read that confession finds a place at the table of healing:

> [13] Is anyone among you suffering? *Then* he must pray. Is anyone cheerful? He is to sing praises. [14] Is anyone among you sick? *Then* he must call for the elders of the church and they are to pray over him, anointing him with oil in the name of the Lord; [15] and the prayer offered in faith will restore the one who is sick, and the Lord will raise him up, and if he has committed sins, they will be forgiven him.[16] Therefore, *confess your sins to one another, and pray for one another so that you may be healed.* The effective prayer of a righteous man can accomplish much." Emphasis mine—James 5:13-16 (NASB)

Suffering can be the result of a disaster, like a car accident or an unexpected disease, but is often caused by our own behaviors and choices. James' reference to being cheerful reminds us that good happens in our lives too, and we are to recognize this and praise God. James then mentions that those who are sick should call for people to pray for them. The implication here is that the responsibility falls on the one who is sick to ask for prayer. In other words, if you have a need be *accountable* to others for the need in your life. Note, however, the process of praying for healing includes the confession of sins, healing of the physical body, and the forgiveness of sins involved. The confession is key, though, because it opens the spiritual door for the body to be healed, and for the mind to be at peace.

We in the church discount confession too often, because it entails absolute honesty on our part. It means the embarrassment of speaking our darkest secrets out loud, and facing the shame related to our behavior. It is nevertheless a crucial part of our spiritual development and Christian maturity. Without it we can never really be honest with God or ourselves. This is why the accountability partner you choose must have strong character, and the willingness to confront you with regard to your sins. They need to encourage you and coach you along, but they also need to be prepared to get in your face when they see you are not addressing the issues at hand.

I have had over two hundred people say they would like to be an accountability partner with me, but I have only had eleven send back a report of how their week went. Later in the book I will share some actual weekly reports I have sent to my partners. You will see they are revealing, cut and dried, and very honest about how my week has been. I share the prominent temptations I faced that week, the struggles I had with people, physical moments of distress related to my diabetes or how I felt at the time, concerns regarding my family, and situations in my church. The report is not always the same, and there are some things I deal with weekly and some I don't. My friends are able to see my heart clearly and know how to pray. They can also ask how I am dealing with any given situation from two months ago.

Being accountable to the law is to drive the speed limit, obey the rules of the road, and pull over when you see emergency lights coming up behind you. Accountability in a relationship is agreeing to let someone else know your struggles, your weakness, as well as when and where you have failed. It is much more though; it is also a sounding board in victory, a request for wisdom, and the cementing of a friendship that will be a cover and guard for both parties. This is why you have to be willing to share the deepest secrets of your soul, to speak your weaknesses in confession, to recognize where you need help in your walk with God.

Humans are proud creatures so we do not easily lower our defensive walls for inspection, which is why accountability goes against our very nature. It fights against our will and cries out in defiance of righteousness for the secrets to remain securely hidden. Accountability requires confession and an absolute assessment of your thoughts, your words, your actions, and even the kind of sin you lean toward. When we keep these things to ourselves, we fight them alone, and typically fail at it. I am not sure where I heard this comment, but it definitely fits in this context: "The power of sin is in its secrecy." If you alone know the sin you struggle with, you fight the battle and the temptations alone. This is not merely a redundant statement; it seems obvious because we *think* we can fight the battle alone most of the time. If fighting alone worked, the world would be a different, and much better place. You can't *fight* alone, however, because you're not *attacked* alone. Your enemy is ruthless, and he wants to single you out.

For accountability to work, you have to be honest and look beyond yourself. You need to assess and confess where your tendency to sin is. Is it the desire to make yourself better than others? Is your pride unbridled and your tongue out of control? Is your attitude in need of an adjustment? Are you the hypocrite the world sees at work? Hey Pastor, do you judge your worth by the size of your congregation? I know pastors who are jealously bitter over what the pastor one city over is seeing happen at his church, and if that is you, then you need to confess and address that sin.

Are you fighting rampant sexual temptation, violent thoughts, insensitive attitudes toward family or friends, or feeling depressed or even suicidal? Does it feel like you are stressed out beyond your capacity to stay sane, are you flirting with the opposite sex or maybe the same sex and crossing moral lines you swore you never would? Have you felt like giving up on your faith, your family, your friends, or even just yourself? Carefully take

Evaluate whether you are dealing with your sin in any real sense at all.

note of your natural behavior to see how you are sinning, where are you sinning, and why are you sinning. Most importantly, evaluate whether you are dealing with your sin in any real sense at all. In other words, are you running from accountability for the sin you are hiding? If so, you need accountability for your sake, and whether you are dealing with any or all of the sins mentioned above, you need accountability for God's sake.

Chapter Five

Transparency Trauma Part I

Iborrowed this paraphrased chapter title from a book[7] I read when
I first entered into ministry many years ago. As you'll soon be
able to tell, the book had quite an impact on me. Consider the
word *transparency* for a moment, and all this word encompasses.
One definition of transparency is the following: *The quality of being
clear and transparent*[8]. This is a crucial quality in the context of
this book. Another definition of the word is: *the property or state of
being transparent; that state or property of a body by which it admits
the passage of: rays of light so that forms, colors, and brightness of
objects can be seen through it; diaphaneity*[9]. I think this is a wonderful
description of the positive potential of transparency—for accountability
partners, transparency means we share our secrets openly, without
hesitation or fear, which can lead to life-changing epiphanies and
glorious growth. It means we are comfortable drawing back the layers
of skin and muscle to reveal our barest heart to another. It means an
absurd level of honesty—an openness that can even tempt anger if you
really think about it. Yes, there is no doubt that transparency takes guts.

What is the deepest secret you have ever shared with someone? And
likewise, what is the deepest secret anyone has shared with you? Being
a pastor, I do a lot of counseling and I have heard plenty of interesting
and sometimes terrifying things. One of my most memorable was a

confession I'd heard when I first entered the ministry in my hometown of Jasonville, Indiana: a childhood friend confessed he had messed up with another woman and needed to tell his wife what he had done. Nervous, I agreed to accompany him home and support him while he told his wife. I also agreed to counsel them if necessary.

My friend's wife listened intently as he shared the indiscretion that had occurred with one of her best friends. When he was done, I thought it went quite well. Sure, she cried and said she needed some air, but it wasn't the brutally awkward scene of devastation I was expecting. When she left the room it almost felt like a high-five moment because we knew it could have gone a whole lot worse. Little did I know, it was about to get worse than I could ever have imagined.

I sat on the couch while my friend relaxed in his recliner when, true to her word, his wife returned to the living room a few minutes later... except she now wielded a large caliber handgun and her eyes were filled with fury. She walked right up to my friend, aimed the gun, and fired three shots. The blast of a .40 caliber handgun only seven feet from your ears is a life-changing moment. I can only thank God my friend's wife was barely behind the line of murderous rage because she had blown three nickel-sized holes in the wall just above his head.

She proceeded to yell and scream and called him every name in the book (some of which I had never heard before,) while pacing the floor like a caged tiger, glaring wild-eyed at both of us. She fixed her eyes on me and I realized from the angle at which I was looking up at her, that I was on the floor next to the couch in the fetal position. Truth be told, I had to make sure I hadn't wet my pants. "Thanks for coming," she growled. "You can leave now. I won't kill him." She said this retaining a firm grip on the gun with her finger still resting on the trigger, so I left in haste hoping she would keep her word (you know, for the sake of accountability).

She never did shoot her husband, but I learned a valuable lesson during that confession—there is a proper time and place, and an appropriate way, to confront an issue of such gravity. There is also a best approach when confessing a potentially hurtful sin to someone. It is essential to carefully and cautiously consider the manner in which you share such a secret. The reality is certain confessions, like adultery, are going to be more explosive than others. They will leave a deeper scar on the person hearing them, but remember the person sharing the indiscretion is also scarred in the process. Confessing sexual sin of any kind is very private and particularly provocative. It is also very humbling and extremely heart-breaking.

I have heard about crimes and business fraud from decades prior, as well as seeing abusers of many kinds break down mid-sentence. Wives have admitted they truly desired to kill their spouse for abuse or adultery. I have warned people for their safety and even called the authorities several times. I have dealt appropriately with things I heard that warranted arrest and confinement. I simply know this—sin routes us far from the leading of our moral compass. This is why whatever

There is a proper time and place, and an appropriate way, to confront an issue of such gravity.

you may think of it, confession is critical to maintain our humanity, and to prevent the belief that we are better than we really are.

This brings us back to the verse in James[10] encouraging us to confess our sins one to another. The idea of confessing our sins is unnatural and shaming to humanity. It goes against everything within us to reveal to a friend or family member what we have done in the dark. We detest having people know who we really are, from our thoughts to our actions and everything in between. Why? We dislike it because we want everyone to believe we are always good and wholesome, moral and modest, and *better than everyone else around us*. The truth is we are so much further away from the person we project then we will ever admit. We are fallen, we are failing, and we are helplessly addicted to sin, even when we try our very best to follow Christ.

But those chains can be broken and can open up an entirely new universe spiritually, *if* you will commit to gut yourself in front of somebody else.

So, what is the biggest secret you have never shared with anyone on the planet? Did you cheat to get ahead of the class? Did you see someone do something they should not have been doing? Did you lie for somebody to cover for them? Those are pretty benign. Ever been a "Peeping Tom?" Have you ever abused someone from a position of power? The list could go on forever, and I am not talking about stealing candy from a teacher's desk in the third grade. I specifically mean the secrets that could put you in prison, destroy your marriage, make your kids despise you forever, or make your mother deny you are her child.

These are the kinds of secrets that have to come out for accountability to work. I'm sure you are already thinking that only God needs to know these things, and there is a little truth to that... but only a little.

When I was eleven, my brother and I, along with some friends, "broke" into an old cabin one late summer before school started. It wasn't really locked; it had a code master lock on it of which I had been given the combination by the owner years before. We justified our actions because we knew the owner would not mind us going into the cabin, but we also knew he had told us to not go in there between August and September. The owner, who was an avid fisherman and hunter, lived a few hours away. He had always let us use his pond to fish and ice-skate on, he let us shoot bottles with ammunition he supplied, and allowed us to raid his fridge which was always full of bottles of pop. It also contained other beverages I was not interested in.

"Hey Dana, let us in to the cabin so we can get some pop. You know the combination," some older friends suggested. I replied that the owner had asked us not to go in there during the month of August. "Come on, he'll never know we were here," they persisted. My response was much the same but they kept on. My resolve started strong but after about fifty appeals to let them in, I caved. I approached the cabin with my brother and four older neighborhood friends, spun the combination numbers, and opened the door. The older boys went in while my brother and I stayed outside as they loaded up on what I thought was pop. In about five minutes, my friends emerged carrying milk crates full of beer and stronger spirits. I protested and asked them to not do this, but they just kept on going. I knew there was no way to hide the theft from the cabin's owner. I was really bothered by what had happened but I was too afraid and felt too bad to do anything except avoid the guy the next few times he returned to his property.

A few years later I was riding motorcycles with my brother on that man's property when he approached us and engaged in basic small talk. After a bit, he said, "Boys, a couple of years ago I lost some alcohol at the cabin and was hoping you could help me figure out who it was. It was during August so I know it would not have been you boys because you knew August was off limits to anyone being out there. So, any ideas?" He asked the question looking straight at me for an answer. This guy knew my dad had issues with alcohol and that we would never touch it for that reason alone. I swallowed hard and swore to him that I had no idea who it could have been. He scratched his head and talked around the issue for a bit, but he seemed to believe us. Then he left. That was how the story remained for the next three years.

The owner was still coming down every summer when I became a Christian at fifteen. One day I saw his car drive by the house and due to my recent salvation I decided I needed to make the situation right. I was also aware that I owed him some money for what was taken, and since I had a business mowing about twenty-five neighborhood yards, I would offer him some compensation.

The man was very glad to see me and asked about my family and school. Then asked what he could do for me. I looked down and gathered up my courage, then spoke up and told him what had happened that day. I promised him that I truly believed my friends were just getting pop. I showed him the money I brought, offering to pay for the stuff they took. I handed him about fifty dollars.

"Dana," he smiled and waved my outstretched hand away. "I appreciate your offer son, but they took advantage of your knowledge knowing I had given you the combination. So I don't need your money, I just need their names." I had not expected him to ask that. I suddenly realized my confession had just muddied the waters with consequences I had never intended. Since I was brave enough to tell him I let the guys in, I guess he figured I was supposed to be brave enough to tell him who they were. After a little prompting, I finally caved, and he wrote the names down in a little notebook he carried in his front pocket.

A few weeks went by and nothing happened, then a month passed so I figured it had all been forgotten and my older friends had not been contacted. The summer passed, we returned to school, and still nothing was brought up. I, of course, never mentioned that I had done the right thing and told on all of us. Finally, around Christmas, one of my friends told me his dad had received a letter from a guy in Indianapolis. The letter had pictures of my friend walking out of that cabin with a milk crate full of beers. I recognized the location of the pictures and also saw immediately they had been cropped to take me out of the picture. The two brothers and my other two friends received the same letter with their very own copies of pictures of them stealing alcohol from that cabin. The note asked for a hundred dollars from each of them for the theft, that they never return to his property, and that they never again take advantage of what their friends know. Shortly after that, I received my own letter in the mail.

The owner told me in the letter that he had been seriously disappointed in me when I had lied to him after the event. He also told me about the cameras on his property and that he knew my brother and

The weight of guilt can literally make you feel heavier and physically belabored.

I had always been good to him and to the property itself. He explained that he'd had those pictures for several years and had often thought of calling the law and creating trouble for my brother and me, but he respected my dad too much to do that. He liked my family and that mattered, so he decided that if I told him the truth before I graduated high school, he would do something nice for me. After I confessed he cut me out of the pictures and he tried to help the other boys to be honest too.

The day after I graduated high school, the owner of that land stopped by the house on his way to the cabin and handed me a $2,500 check for college in the fall. He assured me I would not have received a dime if I had not told him the truth he had known all along.

I tell this story for several reasons: first, to be aware there are things we have done that people already know about. Delaying our confession can have deep ramifications on others' understanding of our character. It can also have severe impact on our conscience. We often try to salve our conscience by justifying whatever we can to feel better about ourselves, figuring that if we got by with it maybe God has given us some slack. That, however, is never the case. Guilt can quickly age you and make you a bitter person. Holding on to past sins can cause stress, pain, and even weight gain which science confirms[11].

A study[12] I read listed ten things we didn't know about guilt, and here are some of them that apply to accountability: unresolved guilt is a like a snooze alarm going off in your head, constantly reminding you of your sins. It hampers clear thinking and reduces concentration, productivity, and creativity. When plagued by guilt we become reluctant to embrace the joys of life, even resulting in self-punishment. Further, guilt causes us to avoid the person we have wronged and can produce resentment towards them. The weight of guilt can literally make you feel heavier and physically belabored.

> *Unresolved guilt is a like a snooze alarm going off in your head, constantly reminding you of your sins.*

The study does mention a positive side to guilt too in that it can protect relationships, like when you know you should send that Mother's Day card.[13] You might have to drive out of your way to buy it, but in the end your conscience will be satisfied you did the right thing.

On the contrary to the negative aspects of guilt, confession contributes positively towards our spiritual life; it calms emotions and brings great peace to the soul. Consider the classic children's prayer: *Now I lay me down to sleep, I pray the Lord my soul will keep, if I should die before I wake, I pray the Lord my soul will take.* Notice there is no confession of sin, no mention of tax fraud, no anger at the neighbor who lets his pets run free, and no road rage comments... only the assumption that God is the caretaker of the soul. The truth of the matter is that no adult would actually pray like this because they have lived a day in the real world. I believe most adults at the end of the day walk through portions of it, relishing the positive highlights, and remembering with resentment those lesser moments better forgotten.

God has given us powerful tools to deal with guilt, however, which I will discuss in the next chapter.

Chapter Six

Transparency Trauma Part II

L eviticus 7:1-7 tells us God instituted a guilt offering for his people, but take a closer look at Isaiah 53:10 to get a better idea of the reason for a guilt offering:

But the Lord was pleased to crush Him, putting *Him* to grief; If He would render Himself as a guilt offering, He will see *His* offspring, He will prolong *His* days, And the good pleasure of the Lord will prosper in His hand. *Emphasis using underlining mine*—Isaiah 53:10 (NASB)

The guilt offering was an atoning sacrifice, or an obligation and payment as a consequence of a wrong done. Offerings were made for unintentional sins as well, but the reality is that most sins, crimes, and indiscretions, are premeditated and committed consciously. Jesus became the payment specifically for the guilt we carry, and even embrace at times, so we could let it go and be free.

In the New Testament, confession is the key to accountability because when we confess our sins we are declaring what we have done, what we have said, and what we have seen. It is an act of repentance to share the dirt and the filth with another living being long after we shared it with God. I believe this is because we understood the sin was against God Himself. When I share what I did this past week,

I am revisiting the wrong steps I took, remembering my victories, and confessing both to someone who already has an idea of where I struggle. The point is that I need to speak it out or communicate it to someone else, so in the future I will know I will have to do this for every sin I commit going forward. It brings into immediate reality the fact that everything hidden will be revealed (Luke 8:17). When I reflect on my mistakes I am also reminding myself of where and why I messed up. It helps me track and strengthen my weaknesses in the same way a review of notes does before a test.

Confession is the key to accountability.

The Catholic Church has a confessional area where you sit in a room and confess your sins to the priest sitting close by. According to Catholic doctrine, to make a confession one must have a desire to acknowledge the sins of daily living committed through their speech, actions, and even deliberate omissions. These sins must be expressed in confession before a priest, and confession is primarily a step in the individual's intention to return to God and subsequently righteous living. When an individual enters the confessional, he or she can choose to kneel behind a screen or be face-to-face with the priest. The priest will offer words of advice or possibly ask questions before, during, and after the confession. After hearing the confession, the priest will assign a type of penance. The penance might be anything from saying prayers to doing a good deed for your enemy.

According to Catholic doctrine, the purpose of the penance is to diminish temporal punishment. The priest will then speak words of absolution (forgiveness on the part of the church), and the sign of the cross is made. The priest may then finish with a few words of encouragement for the individual. According to Catholic doctrine, the process of confession and penance allows the individual to return to a balanced and Godly life.

I would like to emphasize that penance is a uniquely Catholic doctrine. Most Protestants disagree with the practice as it is a one-way, mandated confession, always before someone in a greater position of spiritual authority (the priest). Further, it can be confused as being works without faith, or muddying the waters by implying that we can justify ourselves with works (penance). I do not believe in the doctrine of penance, but to a degree, the Catholic practice of confession is a good start, although I don't believe it should be mandated, and confessing to a priest or pastor is not required. An accountability partner you select and trust, in a two-way relationship, is what I am advocating.

The purpose of confession, however, is more than just confessing the sin so you are publicly identified as the guilty party. In contrast, it has a lot to do with getting rid of the guilt and the reminders of what was not pleasing to God. There is also a need to vent and to decompress because guilt can wreak havoc on your emotions and plague your sleep. I have seen people weep for a long time after sharing their deepest secrets because the weight had finally been lifted from their conscience. Think about how much easier life would be if we promptly confessed our sins, telling somebody what we had done wrong? The emotional drag would be gone and we would almost definitely sleep better. I am not suggesting life will always be all puppies and rainbows, but it should be easier overall if we are consistently confessing our failures and sharing our burdens of guilt with others, asking them to pray for us in those specific areas.

During the first ten years of my ministry, a pastor friend told me he was facing depression in ministry and needed help. I explained how my accountability model worked and asked if he would find it difficult to share exactly what he was going through. He said he could easily empty his heart, so we arranged a time to meet to first talk about weaknesses.

It went really well until I told him what *my* struggles were. The difficult time in my life and ministry had passed about four months before but it was still fresh in my mind. I was twenty-three and single so I was dealing with loneliness, sexual temptation (doesn't every young guy?), and I had faced depression myself with the extreme stress of being diagnosed with Type 1 Diabetes.

I shared how I was a youth pastor at a church in the community where I grew up so everyone knew who I was, the kind of teen I had been, and how I had lived my life up to that point. When I was done,

I said, "So that is where I am and what I fight during the week." I will never forget what happened next. He simply smiled at me, got up, and left without even saying a word. I followed him through the door trying to engage in further conversation but all I received was a hand up with the palm out. Then he said, "I will never share that deep with anybody. Are you crazy? You just told me things I could use against you if I wanted to. What you just did is not guarding your heart—you just gave it away and I can't do it. I'm Sorry." And he left.

I served at that church for ten years, but my pastor friend ultimately left the ministry, went through severe depression, and eventually became suicidal. He showed up again about six months before I transitioned to another church and asked to talk. He was employed in a park system so he suggested a horseback ride while we talked. He drove us there not saying a word until we were on the horses and had started down the trail. It began with hard swallowing and tears, but he finally apologized for walking out years ago and started telling me his history. He said he'd never told a soul before but he had been abused as a kid. His alcoholic father had beaten him, driving his mother to divorce. He was nine years old when his mother left and that was the last time he had seen her. When he was only seventeen his father was killed in a drunk driving crash. He did not attend the funeral.

For several hours he dredged up every major pain he had experienced in his life; it poured out like pus from a lanced wound and it was likewise not pretty at all. He was caught, undone, and empty all at the same time. We finally stopped at a place near the lake in the park and he stretched. Then he put his hands in the air and started shouting and whooping. This spooked the horses royally at first, but they were tied up and he worked at the park, so I wasn't too worried. Unprompted, my friend began praising and thanking God for his life and his difficult situations. He gave God glory for keeping him from alcohol, mentioned he had found his mother in the last few years, and that he was still alive after he had come so close to killing himself because of his messed-up past. Then he began thanking me for being willing to share my struggles with him all those years earlier, and how terrified he was to think I expected him to tell me the same things. That was the catalyst to the day's shedding of burdens–he had found a friend and could begin the process of unpacking his life of misery and shame, finally getting it off his chest. Immediately he was a better man than the one I knew before. That earlier man was guarded and ashamed, and fearful of what would happen if somebody saw him for what he really was. Confession set him free and instantly gave him a different heart.

Transparency terrifies us because we want to be who we think people believe we are. We hope they never see the tragic flaws in our heart, the cracks in our armor, or the muck and despair in which our thoughts live. In 2 Corinthians 10, Paul deals with having to take our thoughts captive. He was referring in large part to thoughts that weigh us down and accuse us, trying to make us believe we are unredeemable and common. Some

Transparency terrifies us because we want to be who we think people believe we are.

thoughts intend to make us feel nothing we do will ever be good enough to earn God's love or favor. In Ephesians 6:10 Paul said we wrestle not against flesh and blood, and that should be a clue that the spiritual wrestling begins in our thought life.

The trauma of transparency is that it requires sheer intestinal fortitude and near-insane courage to tell somebody the secrets from your dungeon lair. Sins and evils—indiscretions, transgressions, violations, shortcomings, and crimes, occur easily in the flesh but the consequences stay with us, in our heads forever. I have heard plenty of deathbed confessions as a pastor and in my opinion they are always driven by accumulated guilt gnawing on the conscience over a long period of time. I have often wondered if those sins had been confessed closer to their inception just how different things would have turned out for all involved, and how much longer the person could have lived.

As I mentioned before, Jesus said "For nothing is hidden that will not become evident, nor anything secret that will not be known and come to light" (Luke 8:17, NASB). Everything will come out, if even only after our death, but maybe even shortly before. Regardless, it will all ultimately come to come to light at the judgment seat. The longer you wait, however, the more challenging and complicated the mess will become. On top of this, the tentacles of involvement stretch through time and leave a lot more ground to cover because the root has grown deeper and born fruit, affecting more and more lives, more and more deeply.

We would be wise to be transparent right now and at the moment of the transgression. Consider for a moment there was no guilt in anyone's head or heart. Imagine there were no secrets lasting decades that would destroy marriages and families if they came out, and picture honesty being a staple like rice or beans (always in ample supply). What could happen if cheaters confessed on the spot during an exam, or if it were admitted that fraudulent contracts were deceitful before signing? It may not completely change the world but it would impact a significant part of it.

This is *exactly* what accountability can do. We just have to be the ones to start it off.

The problem is that the Gospel is full of examples of transparency, yet we don't emphasize enough that transparency is required of Christians. In John 9, we read how Jesus and His disciples came upon a man who was born blind. The disciples asked Jesus if it was the man's sin or his parents' sin that caused the blindness. Jesus confronted their bad theology with a straight answer—neither the man nor his parents were responsible for the physical disability. Culture at the time held that bad things happened to people as a result of specific transgressions— almost a "karma-like" approach to reality. Jesus dealt with that cultural misconception by directly showing where it was wrong; we need to approach the need for accountability in the same way.

We need to face that we don't have it all figured out, that we do make mistakes, and are flat-out wrong sometimes. A true accountability partner will be willing to confront their partner when necessary, while themselves being transparent. Jesus used the situation as a teaching moment to highlight the disciples' flawed thinking, helping them see things correctly. Your partner will play a similar role but may need to pray about it before responding but they also might need to say something immediately, depending on the error in our thinking or theology. In 2 Timothy 4:2b (NASB) the apostle Paul tells us how we should respond by saying we are to "correct, rebuke, *and* exhort, with great patience and instruction." This type of coaching is a particular requirement in accountability, because my partner will see my situation from a different perspective and will patiently help me to understand that perspective.

We deal with sin issues like anger, lust, negative attitudes, and pride daily. Sometimes we recognize the impact of these sins on our lives and sometimes we don't. Even King David, whom the Bible describes as a man after God's own heart, didn't recognize when he opened himself up to sin. In 2 Samuel we read:

> *"Then it happened in the spring, at the time when kings go out to battle,* that David sent Joab and his servants with him and all Israel, and they destroyed the sons of Ammon and besieged Rabbah. *But David stayed at Jerusalem."* Emphasis mine—2 Samuel 11:1 (NASB)

In this instance, David was not where he should have been. He sent someone else to do the job he should have been doing. While his men were away, David got involved with Bathsheba, the wife of Uriah, one of his elite soldiers who was a trusted friend. After she became pregnant, David had Uriah killed on the front lines of battle in an attempt to cover up his sin. He kept fighting against his convictions and his sin had won it seemed... at least for the moment.

Nathan, God's prophet, then approached David and told him the story of a rich man who took a poor man's lamb to fulfill a business transaction rather than paying with one of the many lambs from his own flock. The rich man could have drawn any number of lambs from his flock, but chose instead to take the poor man's lamb. The poor man had no chance of justice and no way to resolve the theft. We read in 2 Samuel that David's instant and fiery response was to call for justice:

> [5] Then David's anger burned greatly against the man, and he said to Nathan, "As the Lord lives, surely the man who has done this deserves to die. [6] He must make restitution for the lamb fourfold, because he did this thing and had no compassion." 2 Samuel 12:5-6 (NASB)

In the next verse, we read Nathan's swift rebuke, saying to David, "You are the man!"

I need a partner who will rebuke me when necessary, as Nathan rebuked the king. No one is above the law—not a beggar, a film star, politician, or a pastor. If we will not address the issues we have walled up behind false pretense, then we deserve to be called out on them. We *need* to be rebuked and reproved, probably a lot more often than we are. The word "reprove" means to scold or correct usually with kindly intent[14], and we need the reproof of others to keep us on the right path and headed in the right direction. Reproof could literally save us from hell.

From one mindless sin, David ruined his reputation, changed the landscape of his family's future, and compromised the kingdom of God as a leader. His sons Amnon and Solomon inherited their father's sexual failures, his son Absalom led a rebellion with David's chief counselor, Ahithophel, who is believed to be Bathsheba's grandfather, and David's grandchildren split the kingdom. If David had done what he should have and gone to war, the adultery would have been avoided. If he had confessed his sin, murder and likely much of the subsequent fallout could have been avoided. David's violent reputation would still have kept him from building God's temple, but the scarlet stain on his character would have been greatly reduced.

Now I wonder what would have happened if Nathan had resisted the Holy Spirit's urging to confront the king, or if he waited longer than he should have. Getting things out in the open may result in trouble for a time, but the truth will eventually come out anyway.

When I first got into ministry, I lived in an older parsonage with a wet basement and old shelving that housed rusting paint cans. While moving a weight set I used with some of the guys in my youth group, I cut the back of my knee on the old shelving. I cleaned it up, applied a bandage, and continued with my day. As expected, it was a bit sore the next day, but two days later it was really inflamed

Having someone else look at your life situations is necessary because they can see what you can't or won't, or haven't even considered yet.

and hurting. I cleaned out some of the infection, applied a topical antibiotic cream, and hoped for the best. By the following day, though, I could not step out of bed it hurt so badly, and ended up in the emergency room. The doctor soon discovered a tiny piece of the rusted metal in my leg. It was difficult to see, even on a sheet of white paper, but it was the cause of the infection and the great pain I was experiencing.

I knew the area was infected but had no idea why, and this is so often the case in our lives. Having someone else look at your life situations is necessary because they can see what you can't or won't, or haven't even considered yet.

True transparency is required by everyone in a position of leadership. You must be willing to call out things you see, and be willing to humbly accept criticism of yourself. The more honest you are the more honesty you will receive. The more transparent you are about your weaknesses, the more transparent others will be with their own. In all sincerity, you may very well save someone's life or have your own saved because you listened to, or addressed a concern with someone. Even more important, you may save someone's *eternal* life.

Chapter Seven

Selecting Your Partner and a Routine

Have you ever just sat for thirty minutes and watched people? I mean really observed them… trying to figure out from visual cues what their backstory is. Why they are who they are, and the reason they're doing what they're doing at that moment. Observation can be one of the most powerful tools in your spiritual walk. In fact, much of the insight I gained during my life came about by observing others. Observation became a window of discovery for me. I learned to pray by listening to others pray out loud. I learned to read the Bible systematically by studying how others read the Bible and by asking questions. The surprising part was that along the way I also discovered I had inherited certain consistent patterns of behavior in many areas of my life. I had picked up particular phrases to use in different arenas, specific words I heard from family and friends, certain ways of resolving the task at hand. Let me provide an example of what I mean.

A Product of Our Surroundings

When signing my last name—Coverstone—I take the bottom of the last "e" and cross the "t" in a big loop. I would love to tell you I taught myself this little identifying Coverstone mark, but honestly, I got it from my dad. He had signed his name this way on everything, even on his business advertisements and business cards. He never sat down and taught me to sign my last name like this, I simply saw it and unconsciously adopted the method in my own life.

A few years before he died, I asked my dad how long he had signed his name like that and his answer surprised me. He told me that his dad (my grandfather) had signed his name this way, but my dad didn't know why he chose to also sign his name in the same way. He just picked it up and began imitating the signature for no definite reason except the subliminal one. At least two generations had been completely unaware of a deliberate, but innocent choice of signing our last name the same way. We just did it without being asked or taught to do it that way; we simply emulated what we observed.

This is a good example of how we are all in some way products of our environment, our families, our habits, our schooling and education, and even our neighbors. We choose our words, our style of dress, our patterns of speech, and the way we drive based on how we were raised. This is true for what we base our spiritual choices on as well. We even eat in our own world of likes and dislikes based on what we were offered as kids. We pick things up along the way as we grow, and some of these things we never even realize we picked up. Think of how often you have been reminded of a person because of the way someone related did something. It might have been the way they spoke, or how they laughed, how they handled difficulty, or just some mannerism of theirs.

God created us with a need and expectation for order and systems.

One of the reasons we adopt behaviors automatically is God created us with a need and expectation for order and systems. Our day has twenty-four hours, the year typically has four seasons, even our bodies have cycles, and we mature, we age, and we learn. We learn the easy way and the hard way, from our own mistakes and (preferably) the mistakes of others. We learn from what we see and from what we experience.

Here is a secret though—observation pays dividends if we pay serious attention to what we observe. This is where an accountability partner really begins to benefit us. We can't be accountable without someone intentionally observing our life in real time, then speaking into our lives about what they see and what we tell them.

Discipline and Prayer

Making accountability work requires discipline on the part of both individuals. You have to find someone who matches your desire to live a Godly life according to biblical standards, and who will hold you to these standards. Carefully consider the people in your sphere of influence whom you respect and admire for their own spiritual commitments. Determine to find someone who will not let you get by or cheat when it comes to giving it all up in honesty. Look for someone who will treat you fairly, yet will tell you the hard things you will not necessarily want to hear, but must hear anyway. Above all, find someone you can trust to examine your life and your areas of sinful weakness. Find that one person who will pray for you as well, and pray based on your report for that week.

The prayer part is essential, because if you confess your weakness to your accountability partner they must in turn do something positive with what you share. They must be a person you can trust; someone with strong character who would never dream of telling another living soul what you have shared with them. They must be able to reciprocate the accountability by sharing with you their life challenges, with the same kind of honesty.

This joint honesty and openness is extremely important, and full accountability never works well without it. If only one person is being honest in sharing their temptations and weak moments, it then means only one person in the relationship knows the other's secrets. If both do not share openly, one has power over the other and that never works. Even in a mentor/student scenario the mentor may be above the student, but the mentor is striving to bring the student up to the level of mentorship; the ultimate goal is to develop the same patterns in the student to be passed on down the line. The coach teaches the player from his experience, sharing his insight, but the real focus is to increase the player's skills and improve his game.

When trying to define the notion of an accountability partner the words coach, mentor, and trainer come to mind, but a word I feel better describes this concept is a word you might not expect. The term I feel best embodies an accountability partner is "servant." In fact, I like the

The term I feel best embodies an accountability partner is "servant."

term Accountability Servant because it encapsulates the entire purpose of accountability. The friend who reads my accountability report each week serves me by getting in my face over whatever issues I haven't overcome. He also praises my victories, prays for the struggles I am facing, lifts my arms in battle, and helps me secure future victories in the weeks to come. He stands by my side and holds me accountable for my actions, my words, and my life choices. This is true servanthood.

I hold the same sway over the person who shares his secrets with me. I can pray for him because I know his specific temptation weaknesses. I know the challenges he faces in his marriage and with his kids, I know the job stresses he faces, and the things and places he needs to avoid. I know what he is afraid of and I know the demons that show up in his dreams. As he shares his heart with me, I learn who he is and what makes him tick. I know what he fights daily, I know the spiritual enemies he faces. Knowing all this, I fight beside him, turning the fight into two of us against his enemy, instead of him fighting alone. Neither of us fights alone because we fight for and with each other.

Not against Flesh and Blood

I'll be frank, fighting alone against a supernatural entity is usually a recipe for disaster. We think we are stronger than our enemy and it is true we are stronger than the enemy through Christ who strengthens us (Philippians 4:13) but we all have blind spots, especially when it comes to relying on Jesus. We mistakenly believe that years of following Jesus makes the fight easier. It's not, because on new levels you encounter new devils, and this is true whether we have truly walked the walk or not.

Ephesians 6:12 (ESV) tells us

"For we do not wrestle against flesh and blood, but against the rulers, against the authorities, against the cosmic powers over this present darkness, against the spiritual forces of evil in the heavenly places."

These are the entities every man, woman, and child on this planet will fight. For some reason we consider ourselves to be in the same league with, and able to fight those said demonic forces, even Satan himself. This is why so many people think they can quit some specific sin cold turkey whenever they want to.

I need help in my fight because my enemy is masterfully deceitful, more experienced, is supernatural, and has a lot more history to draw from. He deceived a third of God's holy angels, and he has successfully tempted the best of God's people throughout the centuries. Some were sadly defeated to the point they never recovered, nor overcame their sinful nature. In spite of being clearly outmatched, we choose to keep our sins to ourselves, to never share our secrets, and to fight these wicked supernatural forces alone. This is why I need a partner who will come to my aid in the battles I struggle to win. That battle partner keeps me honest and has my back in the truest sense. He is someone who runs to my aid when I am outnumbered and outgunned, and fights with me like his life depends on it too. It may well have even been his fight at some time in his life, which is why he fights for you in this way. He understands the battle, and knows the shame and frustration of losing that fight by himself, but since he has been there he probably knows how to beat that level. He is fully aware of how critical it is to win that battle, and because of this, he fights for you to win too.

The accountability servant goes to war for his friends and those he loves. Because he is a servant, he knows the secrets you carry but views you no differently. He holds those secrets close to his heart and never shares them outside of your conversation. The accountability servant is the friend that, like Jesus, sticks closer than a brother, and does this because we need a friend like that. Accountability is biblical and it is practical, but most of all it is necessary.

We all are weak, but deny it. We all struggle, but refuse to be honest and share that struggle with anyone. Once again, the power of sin is in its secrecy. You are fighting a spiritual enemy, which is why you cannot be the only one who knows your weakness and sin. Satan is a very complex strategist who despises you for being created in God's image. His hatred drives him to steal from, kill, and destroy anyone who is striving to live for Christ. If you are striving to live for Christ, make no mistake, you have a very real and active enemy and you need a friend beside you to resist that enemy.

So, choose carefully and choose wisely. Find someone who is not afraid to ask hard questions. Find someone who will keep you on the straight and narrow. Somebody who is willing to hurt your ego and not be afraid to offend you in any sense, but someone who will also do so in love and celebrate your victories. I hope by this point you have a list of people you are considering for the role of accountability partner, so let's go on to flesh out what accountability looks like in a practical sense.

Functional Accountability

Every Sunday afternoon I sit down and write out my accountability report. Call it an event log, a list of wins and losses, or a letter of victories and defeats, but it is simply what my life has looked like since Monday of that week. I share the struggles I have had with other people as well those I have had with my family. I share the temptations I have faced, and areas that need work emotionally, mentally, physically and spirituality. I list my experiences in three specific topics: personal, family, and church.

You can modify your report to fit your particular needs, but this is what works for me so I offer it as a guide. If I ever have a separate struggle that becomes menacing or frustrating, I simply add another column and start sharing on that. The important thing is you share what you need to share and don't hold back. Every man faces temptation in various avenues and alleys, and has different opportunities for sin laid before him. Personal choices and familiar demons will either prepare you to spill your guts, or fight it all alone as you have already tried before.

So, you have a friend or two picked out, you have discussed the accountability partnership with them and now you just need to figure out how it will work best for both of you. When I first needed someone to talk to I was a youth pastor and had recently gone through an exhausting emotional event. Most people have the misguided idea that all pastors have it together at all times in every way. The simple truth is it's not that way at all. Like every other person—Christian, agnostic, or heathen—we are complicated and flawed. At the time, I needed someone in person who could easily read my poker face and address what I tried to hide. I needed that person to be painfully aware of my struggles with loneliness and depression, and with my recently diagnosed type 1 diabetes. What I needed was someone to force me to be honest, so a face-to-face partnership was necessary for me at the time.

In contrast, what works for me now is a weekly email where I share the significant temptations, frustrations, and challenging events of the past week. Through the week I make notes on my phone or in a notebook, with bullet points and emphases where required. On Sunday afternoon, I sit down and open a Microsoft Word document, type the word "Personal" on the page, then consult my notes to cover all the information needed. Typically, this ends up being between four and seven paragraphs and covers my week of issues, stresses, and concerns.

Once I complete the first topic, I start a new paragraph titled "Family." I share struggles with my wife and kids, as well as worries and concerns I have for the futures of my children. As I write this, I have just dropped off my seventeen-year-old daughter in Minneapolis for college, then turned around and drove eighteen hours back home. She graduated from high school a year early, and you can rest assured my friends heard all about my worries and concerns regarding her move to college in the months leading up to her leaving. My daughter grew up driving in Burkesville, Kentucky where there are less than 7,000 people in our county, and now she drives in a city of 400,000 people! Those concerns appeared repeatedly on my list because it was a part of my family dynamic.

I also share the strife I cause with my wife and some of the arguments we might have had, as well as the stress points we experienced in the week (especially when I have done something stupid.) I simply speak it frankly and honestly because our marriages and our kids are not off-limits in personal accountability. They are actually of front-line importance and more than worth your honesty.

The third subtitle I write on my report is "Church." Since I have current board members as accountability partners, I can't adjust the attendance number or enhance what happened in the service that day because they were there. I do, however, share the building struggles, the attendance, the financial issues, but then I also share the great things happening in the church. The reason I share this with them is because my role is pastor, and leading the church is my job, so I talk about it in the context of accountability.

We all deal with work-related stress and challenges so our work is a necessary area of our lives to address. I don't necessarily discuss

Our marriages and our kids are not off-limits in personal accountability. They are actually of front-line importance and more than worth your honesty.

member problems, but I have let my accountability partner know if my wife suggested I be careful around certain ladies. Being a woman herself, my wife will pick up on some cues I will miss. Why is reporting on church issues so important for a pastor? Well, it is crucial my board members see my humanity, and personally, I need to practice humility and a high level of transparency. More significantly, I need them praying for me regarding these matters.

Start off by seeing what works for both of you and what the schedule needs to be, then reassess as required. Change it up if you need to, but it is vital to stay consistent. Weekly meetings or reports are better than monthly, and although daily is nearly impossible with our full schedules, it can be done if the challenges being faced require it. If you or your partner is going through a potentially life-changing crisis, it might not be a bad idea.

The consistency is what matters because your partner needs to know your weekly activities and struggles. If you wait longer than a week, you will forget the details you need to address. I suggest using the notes application on your phone, an MS Word document, or anything at hand to record the highlights of your week. Once a week is the minimum I would advise and if you are struggling with something specific, more contact should be worked out for that particular issue. I still do face-to-face meetings these days, but not nearly as often because my friends know the door is always open for contact. Meetings started off in person until patterns were established, boundaries set, and we became comfortable with the format, then it simply developed as it needed to.

As I am writing this, I spent the day in Egypt with a team of ministry friends visiting the pyramids and the Sphinx. Touring these iconic landmarks was rather impressive but it involved a hectic travel schedule which messed up my usual Sunday afternoon writing and sending reports. I left on Saturday, so on Friday night I did my weekly report and emailed it before I left Saturday morning. I knew I would be on the way out of the country by the time they received my report, but my partner's prayers for me on this trip were far too valuable to wait until I got home to send it. Some of the challenges I faced last week were related to the trip, so their prayers were more important than packing before I left. I was entering new territory with different spiritual ground to traverse so I needed them to pray for me while in Egypt with that in mind.

Create a Schedule Then Make It Work

This is how I recommend you do your first accountability session: select a friend then make the time to be accountable. Meet one-on-one at first and simply talk about your main struggles and temptations. Talk about your marriage, your family, and be honest about what needs work because that is the "iron sharpening iron" part of the process. Talk about job stress and disappointment when it hits. Talk about what or who makes you angry, and discuss when

The real issue with failure is we don't tell anyone when we fail, and this leads to a recurring cycle of failure.

and how you need to be bolder in dealing with people. Talk about everything, but determine which areas you especially need to be accountable for. Then be honest in these areas. The real issue with failure is we don't tell anyone when we fail, and this leads to a recurring cycle of failure.

Recurring cycles of failure in a leadership position can be devastating to a church body. I have been a full-time minister since 1991 when I replaced a youth pastor in my home church. Sadly the former youth pastor became sexually involved with a youth sponsor. A board member in that church helped me stay faithful and focused while serving there, and is one of my accountability partners today.

I served there for ten years then went to another church with a history of moral failure. This church had thirty-two pastors in the ten years I had been a youth pastor in that first church. It should have come as no surprise that when I approached certain men in leadership regarding accountability, they immediately accused me of wanting to know their secrets. I explained that I expected nothing from them except their prayers, but not a single one agreed to the accountability partnership. I approached other leaders in the church and they all turned me down except one. To this day that man remains one of my best friends in the world even though we live five hours away from each other. Accountability works, and has worked for me for over fifteen years now. It might take time, but you need to be determined to make it work at all costs.

Meet and agree on a schedule that works best for both of you then make it consistent, because walking away from this guaranteed positive impact on your life is dangerous for you and those around you. Understand that accountability is a biblical requirement, as well as a personal requirement if you are to live a Godly life. It is an investment in yourself and in others. It is an investment in your marriage and family, because it keeps you honest in your relationships and helps you be transparent at home and outside the home.

Contact might be via email or FaceTime. It might be a sit-down lunch once a week, or more frequently if required. It might be a daily text or even be a thumbs up or thumbs down approach. In one church I served, there was a man who struggled with pornography.

Every Sunday, when he saw me he would either give me a thumbs up, meaning he had overcome that specific issue during the week, or a thumbs down, meaning he had not. He was a very shy gentleman who was extremely embarrassed by his struggle. This was the best way for him to express his situation and the easiest way for me to assess it. By just this visual cue I instantly knew if he needed more prayer or if he was overcoming the situation through accountability.

The reality of accountability and transparency—having someone you can share everything with—is that it is demanding at times and always humbling, but it is certainly necessary. Accountability will make the difference in your life when it comes to sin, especially the sins that plague you more often than others and can ruin your walk with God or your marriage. Achieving real transparency will get easier over time, but I recommend the first time you talk with your partner make it face to face, as emailing or texting them could be an absolute shock to their system. Tell them your biggest struggles, be they power demands, lust, negative attitudes, porn, anger, or anything causing you to stumble in your walk with God. Share how these things impact your marriage, your kids, your family, your job, and your name in the community and church. Find the friend, establish the time, and start tearing down those walls you have hidden your sin, weakness, and fears behind for so long .

Now let's talk about why you have to do that.

Chapter Eight

For Pastors and Those Who Know Them: Part I

Ihave been preaching since the age of sixteen and serving full-time as a pastor since 1991. During that time, I have been a Youth and Children's Pastor, a Worship and Small Groups Pastor, and I currently serve as Senior Pastor. I have spent the equivalent of five full months in a church van, compiled over 25,000 pages of sermon notes, preached thousands of sermons, read over 10,000 books, and have been covered in various substances (like chocolate pudding) raising money for missions because missions is a passion of mine. I have been fully immersed in all things ministry—Bible studies, video studies, Bible quizzes, conferences, this fad and that, but in all those years of ministry I have never once heard a single person say accountability is necessary for ministry.

Pastoral ministry is something only other pastors can fully understand. Pastors are an exclusive group of people who understand long hours and very few pats on the back. We are on call 24/7, expected to know the answer to every Bible question, and expected to show up at a hospital when a church member's family or friend is in the

ER or dying. We are called to schools to counsel the children when a tragedy involving a student occurs. We attend sporting events for the kids in our church, buy from every fundraiser in the county each time we are asked, and know more deep, dark, secrets about people than we could ever share. We have insight into marriages, the addictions of sons and daughters, medical revelations within families, even their life expectancy. We hear confessions and we share the grief of those who have lost someone they love.

Most pastors are fully committed to helping their flock develop spiritually and grow in the grace and knowledge of Christ. When we decided to go into ministry we knew sacrifices would be required and

There is a tremendous price we pay for serving Jesus in full-time ministry.

that from a financial perspective we might be looking at being bi-vocational. We were fully aware that some people would mock our calling, and that many of our peers would leave the calling long before they expected to. A statistic published recently suggested that only one in ten pastors will actually retire as a pastor[15]. In other words, most don't last that long in ministry. This hurts me personally because I love pastoral ministry and cannot imagine myself doing anything else in life. Yet, I also know the stress and strain ministry brings on those called. I know what their families have to face daily and how that builds up over time. I believe all pastors want to see lives changed and souls saved but there is a tremendous price we pay for serving Jesus in full-time ministry.

If I had not gone through the difficult situation I faced right out of Bible College, I probably never would have dug into accountability like I have. I had to because my emotions were frazzled and my heart was deeply wounded. With a new medical situation shaking me to my foundations, I found myself depressed and worried, and there was nobody I knew who had ever gone through my specific trial. I felt alone, and even more than alone I felt entirely abandoned and lost. I was emotionally spent so I have to wonder where I would be today if my friend had not been available to help me when I called. What would I had done if my friend had pushed me away or had been too busy to talk or get involved? I don't even want to think about that. Thank God I am in a much better place now than I was then simply because I had an accountability partner.

Many members of the clergy do not have the same opportunity I did, however, which is easily demonstrated with some insights and statistics I would like to provide. The following statistics regarding pastors and their families reflect the reality of working in ministry. Quoting a news article[16] published in 2010 Pentecostal Theology[17] states that "Members of the clergy now suffer from obesity, hypertension, and depression at rates higher than most Americans. In the last decade, their use of antidepressants has risen, while their life expectancy has fallen. Many would change jobs if they could."

Several more alarming statistics were revealed in the article:

- 13% of active pastors are divorced.
- 23% have been fired or pressured to resign at least once in their career.
- 25% don't know where to turn when they have a family or personal conflict or issue.
- 25% of pastors' wives see their husband's work schedule as a source of conflict.
- 33% felt burned out within their first five years of ministry.
- 33% say that being in ministry is an outright hazard to their family.
- 40% of pastors and 47% of spouses are suffering from burn-out, frantic schedules, and/or unrealistic expectations.
- 45% of pastors' wives say the greatest danger to them and their family is physical, emotional, mental, and spiritual burnout.
- 45% of pastors say that they've experienced depression or burnout to the extent that they needed to take a leave of absence from ministry.
- 50% feel unable to meet the needs of the job.
- 52% of pastors say they and their spouses believe being in

pastoral ministry is hazardous to their family's well-being and health.

- 56% of pastors' wives say they have no close friends.
- 57% would leave the pastorate if they had somewhere else to go or some other vocation they could do,
- 70% don't have any close friends.
- 75% report severe stress causing anguish, worry, bewilderment, anger, depression, fear, and alienation.
- 80% of pastors say they have insufficient time with their spouse.
- 80% believe that pastoral ministry affects their families negatively.
- 90% feel unqualified or poorly prepared for ministry.
- 90% work more than 50 hours a week.
- 94% feel under pressure to have a perfect family.
- 1,500 pastors leave their ministries each month due to burnout, conflict, or moral failure.

The last statistic has been the source of some debate over the last ten years, but having talked to men and women on the front lines I believe it accurately reveals what pastors face daily. I personally know of sixteen ministry friends who have permanently left the ministry in the last two years alone. These are people who served across various denominations and fellowships, and who I have known for at least twenty years. Some are married and some single, with kids and without, some left good churches and some fled from rough ones, but every one of them had a painful story and they each had deep scars. Without exception they all wanted out.

I asked these friends who they had to talk to when things got ugly along the way—with whom they shared their temptations and to whom they vented. It was an easy answer for each of them—they all replied "No one." In ministry there is a joke about the "Lone Ranger" pastor who thinks he can manage all on his own, and who never connects with anybody else. It is expected he will be shot in the field, likely in the back, and he will never see it coming. The harsh reality of that joke is the majority of pastors already have the Lone Ranger mentality, as they are not being accountable to anyone at any time. They rarely share their temptations with people—they don't share their hang-ups, their idiosyncrasies, or their sin habits with anyone. Most of you who are pastors know I am preaching to the choir. As a result, pastors miss out on sharing their struggles and burdens as well.

While writing this chapter I read an interesting article[18] about stress in the workplace based on a published survey[19]. One point that caught my attention said: "Interestingly, nearly half of respondents who admitted to being stressed at work also said they didn't actually end up doing anything to fix the issue. Instead, they simply hoped the problem would go away." Another comment that might interest pastors was, "Predictably, Monday was listed as the most stressful day of the week." There are two takeaways I see in this: The first being we have an enemy who will not relent and whose entire purpose is to push us to quit or fail. The second insight is since most people dislike Mondays, pastors are not alone on this day when we question our calling and value in ministry. Monday can sometimes be a hard start to a long week and pastors understand that Sunday is the ramp up or the downslope for the day that follows.

The majority of pastors already have the Lone Ranger mentality, as they are not being accountable to anyone at any time.

Now I want to address the pastor reading this chapter: How stressed out are you at the moment? What was the most stressful time you have faced in ministry, and is that time still impacting you today? How often have you wanted to quit? How many times has serious conflict with leadership left you weak and bewildered? Has your prayer time and devotional life ever been so dismal or even non-existent that you really didn't care? How many times have you engaged in compromising thoughts, sinful internet viewing, or other activities, and hoped no one ever finds out? If this is you… you are not alone.

A few weeks ago my wife and I went through an extremely

frustrating financial situation that left me very angry. It occurred on a Friday so it could not be resolved until the following week. It involved our bank accounts, an agency that had not done its job, and a debt we were paying off. The gist of the situation is two medical insurance companies, affiliated with churches at which I had served, had filed for bankruptcy, and I was left holding a huge debt. Trust me when I say it was enough debt to have lost a lot of sleep over in the past ten to fifteen years. I slept very little that night and woke up the next morning with a thought I had never had before: Maybe I am ready to quit.

As I've mentioned I have a few really good friends I share my accountability reports with so I told them of my frustrations around the financial issue. To give you some background, my wife works so we can have health insurance as the church I currently pastor cannot afford it. I give at least fifty hours a week to the ministry, and most weeks it is over sixty hours. I am on call 24/7 to pray, counsel, deal with grief, and attend basketball sectional wins, weddings, funerals, and more. I meet people for breakfast and lunch to discuss church situations, ideas, events, and to help them in their decision-making processes and life challenges. I face stressful situations in the church and community setting often on a daily basis, plus I have to carry many of my congregation's individual and family personal pressures. In other words, my life is my ministry—it is stressful but it is not just me; every pastor lives this out every day.

All pastors have to address the issues they face. We are tempted, we are exhausted, and we are overworked and underpaid for the most part. We deal with leadership expectations around growth and finances and community involvement expectations that are often impossible to achieve. We have financial struggles no one in the church can imagine. As a youth pastor I received a Red Lobster gift card from a family in the church one Christmas. My wife and I were thrilled to receive it and looked forward to eating at the restaurant because at that time it was a restaurant above my pay-grade. The night finally arrived, and while we were eating an older man from the church approached our table. He asked us what we were doing there, specifically saying, "I didn't think we at the church paid you well enough to eat at Red Lobster."

This gentleman was known for his needle-sharp comments and critical spirit so I took the comment with a grain of salt. He approached a church board member the next Sunday, however, and demanded to know how much I was being paid. He was informed that the salaries and benefits of staff are revealed at the church business meeting and that if he had ever been in attendance he would know the figure. He then declared, "Well, if we are paying him enough to eat at Red Lobster, we should pay him a whole lot less." When I heard this, I was deeply hurt in my spirit. Instead of seeing the sixty hours a week I put in with youth and children, the weeks of camp I worked every summer, the discipleship programs I ran with students, the services I delivered every week, and the countless hours of meaningful ministry, all he saw was my wife and me eating at a restaurant I was not worthy to eat at on his tithe money.

Then there are the notions around what vehicle a pastor should be driving. In Terre Haute, a man stopped by the church one afternoon and wanted to meet me. He told me he had formerly attended the church, but had a bad taste in his mouth from previous moral failures in that particular church. He only had one question for me though, and it really surprised me when I heard it. He wanted to know what kind of car I drove. I asked him why that was important to him. He stated simply that he believed a pastor was supposed to drive a nicer car, like a Lincoln or a Cadillac. I was driving a Saturn at the time, which did not qualify as acceptable to him. I know—an unexpected twist, but it goes to show you that the opinions come from everywhere, and they are often not rational.

Conversely, my wife and I were grilled over a new car we purchased in 2007—the first new car either of us had ever bought. Working for a school at the time, my wife was making the payments on the car but some people in the congregation were still upset we had a new car. To be fair, others in the church were thrilled we did but some still felt we should live "humbly" as pastors. This interpretation of humility meant no new things, no nice things, and no material thing indicating any kind of favor from the God we served (they probably would have been mad at the Red Lobster gift card too). There were a few who felt we should have the best, but their reasoning, though, was to show off our church.

This is the kind of ridiculous tightrope pastors must walk when they least expect it, and when people's expectations are made clear. My goal here is to both show lay-people what pastors go through, and to encourage pastors that you are not alone. Most important, however, my goal is to show pastors that you need to have an accountability partner to be a check and balance and an encouragement when storms arise.

Let's continue to see some of what pastors face from their own congregations, and how to manage that accountability.

Chapter Nine

For Pastors and Those Who Know Them: Part II

Our congregations are not always nice to us so don't think pastors are exempt from unforgiveness issues either. We know up close and personal how painfully sheep can bite. I have another true story to illustrate this: My wife and I were expecting our first baby and were beyond excited to share our news with the congregation. We announced it on a Sunday morning and received great support, congratulatory comments, and heartfelt hugs. The next Sunday as I was shaking hands with some of the early Sunday school attenders, I was shocked by an older saint who I immediately wanted to slap when I heard what she had to say. I am not kidding either. This woman had been a friend of my grandmother and I had always respected her because she had been decent to me to that point.

She shook my hand and said, "Do you want to know what I think about you having a baby?" I smiled, expecting her to say something about my grandma being proud or happy. Instead, she said, "I think you are a fool to have a baby, because all you are doing is bringing another diabetic into the world." I was stunned by the statement's insensitivity and meanness. I honestly struggled to recover and say anything resembling kindness.

I grumbled through a youth class I taught that morning, then in kid's church we just watched a Veggie Tales video because my ability to function was gone. I was so angry that I sat in the pastor's office that afternoon venting about how ready I was to break that woman's neck for what she had said. It wasn't just hurtful, it was deeply personal and ridiculously insensitive, and I had to live with it. I spent several weeks flat out mad at the woman. (Excuse my honesty, but this a book about transparency and accountability, right?)

I have many more accounts of painful exchanges, impossible expectations, and even outright betrayal by leaders and friends. Once, I was sold out by a church board who had met privately to remove me as the chairman. The board had met secretly with a staff member and believed some very convincing lies. They took my keys and church cards, and told me they would box up my office and deliver it to my home in the following two days. Six men shook my hand, hugged me, and led me out the door, all with smiles on their faces. They gave me a signed contract with guarantees of full pay and health insurance through to the end of the year, even if I was hired elsewhere before then. They then broke the contract when I was hired at another church three months before the end of the year. They had even included in the contract that I was not to contact the District Superintendent about what had happened.

That transition sent both my wife and me into serious depression. It hit my family very hard and it disrupted everything in our lives. It took me years to emotionally heal from that event and it deeply wounded my family leaving several scars from it all. The district even sent us both to Emerge Ministries for counseling due to the brutality of what had happened. We eventually healed and with a lot of patience and accountability went on with life. About seven years later, however, that staff member and an accomplice were found to be involved in illegal activity and were removed from the position in the church. Right after this happened over twenty people whom I had pastored at the church contacted me to let me know that they no longer believed anything the congregation had been told about my departure. Thankfully this brought my family some closure.

These stories are only a few of the many heart-rending experiences I have endured in this life called ministry. You can imagine the emotions, the pain, the things I wanted to say, and the faces I wanted to punch throughout some of those encounters... but I had a reputation to uphold, a calling to confirm, and a testimony to keep. It was hard to keep a straight face when I was dying inside and wanted to lash out. But you just do it.

You can pour into a family or individuals for months and years and suddenly they just leave and go somewhere else, or no church at all. You can go to the hospital at three in the morning to meet parents who just lost a teenage daughter to a drunk driver and grieve with them, then watch them blame God for it and walk away from their faith. You can do funerals where only two people show up because of the character of the person who died, then have people in your church get mad because you performed the funeral to begin with.

Everything you do is judged and evaluated a thousand different ways, and this is why ministry is both demanding and demeaning. You hurt while you do it and get hurt while you are doing it, but this makes you especially thankful for the victories along the way, no matter how big or small. Ministry is hard, it hurts, it works your soul, it fights your mind and your spirit, it wears you out, but I couldn't imagine doing anything else.

So if you're a pastor, I know there is a lot going on around you and a lot going on in your head which means these are just a few of the necessary questions to ask:

- Who in your church catches your eye because of specific, attractive body features?

- Who you could become familiar with if you're not careful?

- Who in your church has hurt you and you have not really forgiven yet?

- Who is the other pastor in town who intimidates you because of their success, or the numbers in attendance at their church?

- What are you doing in your private time that is close to being unacceptable, or crosses that line?

- Where do your thoughts run to and how hard is it for you to take them captive?

- Is your time in prayer and reading the Word as frequent as it should be, or is it even non-existent?

- How are you addressing your personal temptations, if at all?

Pastors are individuals with a unique calling—a calling that draws the enemy's focus. Pastors are not above anyone else but people often

> *This call demands that we stand before people every week declaring the way to live, all the while struggling to live that way ourselves.*

elevate us because of what we do and Who we represent. This happens because of the life-changing nature of ministry and the impact it has on people and communities, so it makes perfect sense that those behind the pulpit are targeted for failure. James, the head of the early Church, has this advice: "Not many of you should become teachers, my brothers, for you know that we who teach will be judged with greater strictness" (James 3:1, ESV). There is a very important reason this verse highlights a warning to those who would accept this call—this call demands that we stand before people every week declaring the way to live, all the while struggling to live that way ourselves. This call requires us to live above the superior expectations of those who watch us, who follow our steps, and who try to imitate our lives in specific ways. After all, we are at all times expected to be the example in every area of morality and behavior. This is perhaps the greatest strain and struggle of being a pastor. We have to be perfect at all times, even when we are not, while we know better than anyone else that we are far from the expectations thrust upon us.

Pastors also have to live with these words of Jesus in mind: "But whoever causes one of these little ones who believe in Me to stumble, it would be better for him to have a heavy millstone hung around his neck, and to be drowned in the depth of the sea (Matthew 18:6, NASB)." The thought that your mistakes, whether unintended or not, might cause another life to explode or fall apart is terrifying. Jesus is not speaking literally about children in the context of the verse; the lesson concerns becoming child-like in faith. It addresses the heinousness of causing believers to sin and to stumble in their faith and walk with Christ. When pastors do not live up to the expected standard fellow believers are part of the fallout and it remains messy for years to come.

If this is not abundant reason to be accountable in our actions and behaviors then I am not sure what is. When your decisions can become the reason some people will walk away from Christ, or possibly spend eternity in hell, it changes the reality of how you live in front of others. This is especially true for your conduct in the shadows. Our choices as pastors can have dire and eternal consequences and we cannot say we had no idea of those consequences because we were warned. One of the best ways to understand the weight of failing as a pastor is to hear it from one of these men personally. I received a call from a failed pastor after he found out my topic for a doctoral thesis was "Following the Moral Failure." He wanted to express the hurt he felt for failing his family, the church, and the families involved. This is a direct quote from that pastor:

"I lost my wife and my kids, will never stand behind a pulpit again for the rest of my life, and I have become the source of laughter and mockery in the community where I served. I have been spat upon and threatened by the husband of the woman I was involved with, told to walk away when I encountered former church family in local stores, and been asked to please move out of the area as quickly as possible by board members. I have seen the wounds I have caused in the tears and in the very looks of the people I hurt. I have seen heads turn away when I enter a room, have witnessed former pastors I knew and worked with not sure how to act once they saw me, so I am very aware I have left a mark that is not good. I am ashamed, but no one believes it, and this is how I will live the rest of my life. In shame. Because even if I could say I was sorry to everyone I hurt, and even if I could muster up the shame I felt for what I have done to my family and my church, even then, few would believe me or take me seriously because of what I had done."

While this statement amazes me more every time I read it, it also brings agony to my soul because of the disgrace moral failure brings. It is more than shame—it is loss. Absolute and utter loss for all involved and for all who are aware of it. The spiritual and emotional investments made in people subsequently rot because they question your loyalty, your walk, and your faith. Worst of all, in doing so they question the same in themselves.

You were the one who was supposed to be an example, but when the forbidden fruit proved too strong a temptation you ate it, and everyone else around you died. Then you die every time the memories come rushing back. As a pastor you must have a game plan to avoid the attacks and moral temptations you will certainly encounter, and to share the many burdens of ministry. You must be accountable and transparent to someone at all times. Find that person who will hold you accountable and keep you presentable. Answer the hard questions. Never walk alone in your wounds nor your fights with temptation. Always share your failings with someone—the secrets you tend to hide. Don't be the one who hangs a millstone around someone's neck because you could not keep a sensible head. Don't fight the temptations alone without sharing your secrets, or you risk leaving a tidal wave of mistakes behind you. Don't be that pastor. Make a decision today to find an accountability partner, and begin the discipline.

As a pastor you must have a game plan to avoid the attacks and moral temptations you will certainly encounter.

Chapter Ten

Accountability on Paper, Part I

Have you ever felt the frustration of trying to follow instructions that are not as clear as you need them to be? I have assembled enough of those boxed, pre-fabricated book cases that my stress level rises at the mere sight of one at a chain store. I always end up with extra parts, or I twist too hard on the soft aluminum rounded cam bolt so that it bent or broke right out. The instructions say to call the 1-800 number if there are parts missing, but not what you should do if you break a flimsy piece in the assembly of the item.

When I was in fifth grade a teacher handed out a test paper face-down. We were told to read the instructions thoroughly and carefully, directions the teacher expressly stated about five times. The instructions were rather silly and juvenile looking back on the exercise but they definitely made an impact on everyone who didn't act on the first instruction. The first instruction was simply stated but very clear: "Please read all instructions 1-9 before starting." "Easy enough" you may say, but considerable embarrassment was involved for those who did not heed that first order. Instructions 2-8 required the students to stand up, say some animal's name out loud, and to walk around the room while whistling or performing a similar action. Instruction 9 said, "Write your name on your paper, do none of the instructions listed above in points 2-8, and turn the paper in." Number 10 was the giveaway, however, as it said, "Because you read the instructions fully and did 9 and 10 only, you will receive an A on the test and a special prize." Most of the class, including me, did not get the A nor the special prize. Only two girls in the class followed the instructions correctly, while the rest of us got chewed out for not first reading all the instructions as we had been instructed to do. Little did we know other teachers as well as the principal were in the hallway watching us demonstrate our rebellion of "not reading instructions."

Sometimes our decisions can seem very foolish to those who know us. To keep from appearing foolish always read the instructions before you start something. As a pastor I have heard confessions of just about anything and everything you can imagine. Often there is considerable shame and many tears accompanying those heart-felt words, as well as sobbing and very deep emotion. It is as gut-wrenching to hear the emotion as it is to watch the transformation as the worst of it comes out. We all make mistakes and we all fail on the journey but what matters is getting back up and fighting the shame of what you have done.

I want you to know that in this chapter and the next I will be extremely transparent as I provide examples of following the instructions well. You are about to read six of my personal accountability sheets which I have sent to my accountability partners over the years. I have kept every single accountability sheet, even the hand-written copies, for a few specific reasons. First of all, I keep them so I can monitor my growth over certain temptations, as well as difficult situations I am working through. Secondly, I am able to monitor just how transparent I am being with those partners (we all know what we leave out). This provides a means to detect where I have improved in my transparency over a month or several months. I will also immediately recognize if I have made no progress, and my partners have the right to ask me about anything I post for the entirety of the accountability relationship. To work properly it has to be this way regardless of the situation.

I am going to share two examples from each church I served at; one from the beginning of my time at that particular church, and one near the end. I have intentionally selected more personal and difficult examples so as to convey the emotional place I found myself in at the time. I share these to show the level of transparency I allow. I was a youth pastor at my home church in Jasonville for just over ten years, pastored in Terre Haute, Indiana, for right around nine years, and am currently a few months into my ninth year in Kentucky. Some of these samples will be shocking as they are brutal documentaries of my life during the period in which they were written, but I needed accountability for where I was at the time. I have provided a little background of what was going on in my life when I sent each report.

Here we go…

I went through a civil and ecclesiastical annulment of a marriage in 1992, right at the start of my ministry career. The woman I had married had dealt with sexual abuse as a child and it impacted her so deeply that the marriage lasted only nine months. The stress of our marriage's disintegration resulted in the onset of Type 1 diabetes in my twenty-three-year-old body and I lost fifty pounds in four weeks. I was an emotional mess, a physical wreck, and I was living it all out in front of my church as their youth pastor. My wife at the time and I had both spent time at Emerge Ministries Counseling Center, and she had also spent several months away from me receiving counsel and trying to heal. The first accountability sheet you will read was written in November of 1992 when I had only one friend I was talking to:

Personal—I am dying and spent. Diabetes is out of control, can't sleep and I have never been this lonely in my entire life. _____ has been gone now for several months, won't talk to me on the phone, won't write and even her parents tell me they are worried about her. What am I supposed to do? I am a married man with a wife that can't be in the same room with me, one that can't even stand to look at me just because I am a man. We had marriage counseling, we stayed pure before we got married, we did it right, and now she has left and will not communicate. I have to work with kids and youth every week that want to know when they can see her and talk with her. And even worse, there are people in my church telling me they understand what I am going through. *Arrrrrrgggggghhh*, they have no idea and I want to strangle them when they say it or just scream NO YOU DON'T because YOU CAN'T! How can they understand having a wife who is working through abuse if their wives never were? They are trying to help because they know me but I hate it. It doesn't help. Nobody knows what it feels like to see your wife be able to hug men in the church, but she can't hug you, can't even be in the same room with you. I know people are praying for me and for her, but there are others who are saying terrible things to me. "You know you missed God and now these kids have to suffer because you didn't listen." "Diabetes is your curse for missing God." "I don't want my teenager around your ministry because any advice you give them on dating and marriage will be hypocritical." I am ready to quit and have just started but feel so little support from anybody. My pastor is there and very encouraging and my family is my biggest strength, but I know absolutely that nobody and I mean *nobody* can possibly understand what this feels like. Who can I talk to and who can I spend time with? There are kids not showing up for activities and teens that are AWOL since it all came out. I am so lonely and tempted and I hate it too. I am a mess and need your prayers badly. I can't see true north and even struggle to pray and read because I feel so empty. My sexual temptations are off the charts, my dreams feel like attacks on my body, and I am so sick from the glucose highs that I am soaking the bed in sweat almost nightly. I am seriously thinking about getting a dog and teaching it Greek commands. I am taking long walks at the state park at night when I can't sleep, but got asked to leave the other night at 3am by one of the DNR guys. I can't even find a place to vent. I have bought a Wavemaster and put it in the basement to hit and kick and it helps, but sometimes I get so mad that my hands are blood covered by the time I'm done. So pray for my anger too because it is out of control as well. Like I said, I am a mess and I hate what I am, even when I am leading worship or preaching to the youth group. Even leading Sunday night worship is killing me because I see faces of people who have questioned my integrity and discernment sitting out there watching me. Ministry is okay for now but my heart is always torn because my mind and body feel so far from these kids I love so much. It is very hard to give a hundred percent when your body and your mind are bleeding at the same time. And my mind is at war every second of the day and night to the point I just want to scream. Devils are liars and all that I am hearing at the moment are lies about me. Just pray that I can sleep and my glucose levels get under control, and that my thoughts become saner than they are at the moment. I am going to explode if I can't get this stuff out. Thanks my friend for standing in the gap for me. November 8, 1992

Frankly, it was one of the toughest years of my life but thank God, I had a friend who helped me carry my burden. It was a tremendously heavy burden but having a friend to help me navigate that difficult time made it survivable. During our accountability sessions I poured out my heart to that friend and he stabilized me for several years. It was him I traveled to see when things first fell apart and it was him who kept me on the straight and narrow. He was at the root of my accountability system. I cannot adequately express my immense gratitude to him for his friendship and compassion for a friend who was at the end of his rope. My friend has requested anonymity for various reasons so this mention is my thanks.

Years later as a youth pastor, I sensed a change in plans for my life and the next entry—about three months before 9-11—gives some reference to that time:

Personal—Got a call this week from a pastor in Terre Haute wanting to meet with me and discuss an opportunity at his church. He had seen me at the Baccalaureate service as a student from his church was present and it was right before the graduation service. Jennifer and I have been trying for our third child for several months now but have also sensed that there may be some transition coming. I have sensed it since about spring break and especially during the commission conference earlier in the spring, so that phone call from the pastor made sense. But the history of that church is well known and it's not good. But wow, I will have been here ten years in August, but believe working with Pastor Bush has trained me to understand ministry better. He has been here since right after I started at CBC and the church is solid and

89

missions giving is solid too. Jen and I have talked a lot about what leaving looks like. We would still be close to family and we both have family in Terre Haute. I really want to make it ten years here though. I graduated from high school here, grew up here, messed up in front of many people here while I was growing up, and I know everybody and everybody knows me. My biggest fear is missing God in all of this, so my prayer life is stronger and my time in the Word has increased to. I have to get this right because Jen and the kids need me to get it right too. A change will mean a bigger school, more opportunities, more places to go, and parks to visit. But have to wonder about a house and if my credit is good enough to even be considered. Since the medical insurance bankruptcy back in 1993, I have been saddled with the huge debt and it might cause me some issues. I will know a few of the particulars next week. Meeting in a few weeks at Red Lobster so I don't even know what will happen. It could fall apart at the seams but who knows what is ahead. Remodeling here at the church parsonage is pretty much done and it is really nice; more room, which helps. I feel bad knowing we might be leaving after the fixes were made, but those needed to be made to begin with.

Family—Keilah will turn four in about thirteen days, and Micah will be two in September. The church loves them very much and takes great care of us. That makes the idea of a move challenging as well. This is all they have known so far. Jen and I have been trying for a third baby and for all we know could be pregnant right now. We would like to have four, but twins right now would be an interesting occurrence considering the timing. For the first time in a long time I am thinking about the next step, and it's been over ten years since graduating with from CBC in 91 and gearing up for seminary. Never got there as I came to Jasonville instead, but it was all God's will. Now I seek my next step and it will impact my family as much as it does me.

Church—Kids church is still going strong, I have great youth helpers and my youth sponsors are the greatest. They give and they give and they give, and they serve beyond description and are so helpful. This last graduation has some of my best teens headed all over the place: college, military, probably a few weddings this fall too. I have watched these kids grow up for almost ten years now in August. That is going to be the toughest part of leaving.

I loved the ten years I served at Jasonville Assembly of God, or JAG as it was affectionately called by many. I did leave my home church in September that year and actually had my first meeting with the staff in Terre Haute on September 11th 2001. That should have been an omen in one sense, but the next two accountability reports are from the next nine years of ministry there. I had been in Terre Haute about eight weeks when the entire staff was told of necessary pay cuts to be implemented within two months. I had just signed a mortgage the week before we were informed of this. This first report is from November 2001:

Personal—Mixed emotions and almost tempted to see if my old job is still available. I will start a fifty percent pay cut next week and have not found a way to make that up just yet. Not even sure where to start. One of the guys in the church said he will talk to his boss who owns a carpet cleaning company, just hoping I can find something and find it soon. Never saw this coming and no forewarning. Told Jen last week and she did not know what to say. Have not said anything to the kids as they would not understand anyway. First house payment in three weeks' time, and now I have no idea how I will pay it and everything else. But God, but God, but God is about all I can say. I don't blame the pastor for this but question why this was not a discussion point when I was hired three months ago. On top of that, there seems to be some disgruntled leaders wanting to get my opinions and information on office activity, which I won't give. I have studied the past of the church and the last several years every pastor has been removed or encouraged to leave. Have some concerns about the board but not sure what they are, just a sense. Very frustrated as I do worship, preaching more than I thought, and Wednesday night teaching, plus leading small groups and doing one myself. Feel stretched and only been here a few months. Biggest stress is finances. Jen has talked about subbing, so maybe I will look at that too, but then it cuts into work days for church work. Everybody took a pay cut, some more drastic than others, but fifty percent is drastic for me. Thursday is my day off so I will be considering options until then for extra work and jobs that will help me pay the bills. Temptations are not too aggressive, although I sense different demons here in the community, and especially at the church. A lot of pride, and there is a marked difference when I walk into the prayer room up in the tower. It is like I am being watched, to the point that I actually looked for cameras. Not supposed to feel creepy in a prayer room but this one does, so I pray in other places. Several families have really accepted us into their lives and that has helped, especially those with kids our kids ages. Jennifer is making friends as well and that is helping her too. But the financial concerns are the biggest hurdle so far.

Family—The kids are loving the new school and we do too. They also love that we live between Dobbs and Deming Park—parks I played in as a kid myself. It feels very comfortable here, the neighbors have all been great, and the kids have good friends at church. Jen and I feel like the rug got dragged out from under us with the pay cut but I took the family out to red Lobster this past week and we talked about the newest Coverstone who will be here in March, and that adds more stress too because of finances. I don't want financial stress to hurt Jens pregnancy either.

Church—Not sure how to feel yet as I see good and bad here as far as the spiritual, and already aware of several wrong relationships and sexual comments and jokes by leaders that concern me. Praying for ways to help. Worship team is really coming together but several of the vocalists have made it clear they will not train others for helping as primary backups. This is both disappointing and selfish and one of the roots of issues in the worship team. Need to know how to handle it and train others for ministry and service.

That was right at the beginning of my time in Terre Haute. I endured those trials and was eventually asked to become the senior pastor which meant facing some rather considerable changes and challenges in the church. The church building was less than fifteen-years old but we had to tear it down due to building code violations and prior bad management. We had received shut-off notices from several utility companies and the church carried a huge mortgage in excess of $750,000. To compound matters there was a serious lack of trust in church leadership. In the ten years I had been a youth pastor at one church, this church had been through *thirty-two* pastors and staff pastors. Added to this, two of the former pastors who had been fired had started churches in the same town and subsequently tried to convince their former parishioners to join them.

As I've mentioned, the church was a mess when I accepted the role of senior pastor but before my family left Terre Haute the church mortgage was down to only $200,000 and I had become their third-longest-serving pastor in eighty years. The next accountability report is from March of 2010. I would be leaving Terre Haute in June:

Personal—Had a lady in my office today who told me she has a way of helping us pay off the mortgage in less than two years, but said she would tell me more closer to the first of summer. Just finished my MA in Expository Preaching with a 3.9 and honors and feeling very good about that. The first MA in New Testament I hardly remember due to the emotional train-wreck, but this has brought a boost of confidence. We have given more to missions than last year, our Church Life model is going well, but a board member has confided in me that several board members are not happy about using our church van to pick up some trailer park kids. I also have been bothered by two board members who are always late to meetings and never pray with us in the secret place before board meetings. It unnerves me because it is constant, and there is never any reason as they were never late before. Trying to watch my attitude as it seems intentional but not sure. My stress levels have been higher too because the board has been meeting on Wednesday nights to deal with finances and I hear very little about the discussions. Our attendance is averaging around a hundred and eight people, offerings are good and my youth pastor had a growing group on Wednesdays as well. Another board member asked me how I, the youth minister, and his wife were getting along and I asked why. He said he was just wondering and making sure things were good there because of some conflict over the last few months. I had been encouraging the YP to branch out and possibly apply to pastor another church in town where he had some background. He had confided in me that he was seriously considering it. Here is my thinking. I see a window of maybe three more years here. I would like to hire a new guy and groom him to eventually replace me, as I sense the timing there. I pray and pray and pray daily, and feel like the walls I am hitting are being intentionally built and that I should be watching my back. Even Jen is telling me that, and one guy who had been on the board and felt he should move on told me something recently when I ran into him. He said be careful who you trust on the board, but would not say more than that. This definitely synced with what I had been feeling in some sense, so not sure what the future holds but now have reason to watch more carefully. What is coming, I have no idea so I wait and prepare for whatever it is. Still seeing people saved and filled with the Holy Spirit and subbing more with the high schools too. Been paying enough to have the twenty-five year mortgage paid in fifteen with additional money from subbing and exactly an extra hundred dollars each month, so at least that is going well.

Family—Jen has been warning me but does not know exactly what to watch for either, just that it involves board members or leaders. It is stressing her, but she is staying busy subbing and working at the schools and loving it. Keilah is going to be a teenager in a few months and I am so proud of her as her grades are solid A's and her accomplishments in school and at church are great too. All three are involved in Bible Quiz, Wednesday night activities, and even worship. Micah is trying to figure out if he is going to play baseball this summer or not, and I'm not sure what is up with that. He has told me he wishes he did not have to wear glasses, so maybe that has something to do with it. It could have to do with the guy that caused so much trouble at the daycare several years ago, because he works there. He also talks to me a lot about the guy that attacked me right after we got here and before we tore the building down. He wants to know the way I put him to the ground and what pressure points I used to keep him there. Not sure if he is afraid of something or someone or what it is, but praying about this as I need to know. Hannah is always smiling and singing, and talks about wanting to get dogs again. She also wants me to make Keilah move into the basement so she will finally have her own room. Funny child she is.

Church—Lots on my mind, and as if that is not enough, wondering who I can trust. Maintenance guy is really making a difference around here and fixing things right and left. I appreciate talking to him some days as he is a great listener and becoming an even greater friend. Gearing up for summer activities and a kids revival in July, may even try to do fireworks as a man has said he would put up half the money to do the show in the church parking lot like they had done years ago. I think we can pull that off.

I left that church in June when it became obvious the board wanted me gone. That led to several months of uncertainty about the future. I cleaned carpets to feed my family and pay the bills and eventually left the state in which I had served for nineteen years of ministry. I put in over forty applications for pastoral jobs in the area before I discovered where God was leading me. At most of these jobs I was told I was overqualified.

The kids started school and I still had a paycheck coming in but my house was on the market and I was at a loss for direction and deeply wounded by men I had trusted. I eventually received a call from the Kentucky Assemblies of God Superintendent who told me they would love to have me there, then told me about a church he thought might fit me well. In October of 2010 I was hired in Burkesville.

Thus began our new life in Kentucky..

Chapter Eleven

Accountability on Paper, Part II

In Burkesville, I began my tenure at a church recovering from a painful ministry situation while I too was still recovering from my wounds, so we were kind of made for each other. In contrast to Terre Haute, however, I had a solid board of men I thoroughly trusted, and a much smaller but friendly community. The stressors were very different however. For the following two years I would deal with paying for a rental home in Kentucky and a mortgage in Indiana, plus utilities in both. It would take almost eighteen months to sell the house in Indiana, eventually having to do it through a short sale to make it happen. The majority of my income was spent on paying for the two homes. I had no health insurance and had to pay $1,600 a month for medication for an insulin pump. It was not easy, but as always, God was faithful. The first report from Burkesville, Kentucky is from May 2013:

> **Personal**—The house is going to sell, the house is going to sell. Thank God, as I signed a document faxed it back through the bank on Friday. I was at a loss to even know what to do and it still

seems unreal. I was in the ER a month ago and got the bill on that today, so our financial pain is not offset but at least the house is being bought. The agent called me at the church and I shouted so loud the custodian came to make sure I was alright. Been subbing a lot and feeling better physically. Been off the pump for over a year now and still have some issues but am trying very hard. The church can't afford insurance but they take care of my family and I appreciate that. I have several ladies who want me to counsel with them and after discussing it with Jen, she was ok with one of them but not the other. I trust her instinct and did as she felt best, and based on the response, my wife was right. Met with the Middle School principal to talk about mentoring young men there and am working to make that happen when school starts in the fall. Very hopeful about this as it does not exist in this area. Have had several aggressive people show up at the church wanting gas, food, rent, money, etc., and they don't like to take no for an answer. Called the police twice this past week after one threatened me. I always carry and have to here, as do several men in the church. Still dealing with lots of people who have been hurt at our church, specifically women, and I hear a lot. Biggest struggles have been my anger and dealing with aggressive people demanding things from the church. My thought life is under control as far as my eyes go, but anger is starting to surface as I deal with people who don't get it.

Family—Jen is doing much better emotionally and loves working at the school, and it is really helping her. The guys praying on Thursday mornings is also really helping Micah grow in the Lord. They are encouraging him and he is talking about ministry and asking lots of questions about what pastors do. Not sure how to handle that but the marks are there, so I want to be very honest about life as a minister. Keilah is talking about dual credit classes and trying to get ahead as soon as possible. We talk lots about her future and what kind of job she is wanting to do, still not sure. Her grades are great and her attitude is too. Hannah is singing like crazy and we can all tell her voice is really a gift and we hear that a lot. When Keilah plays and Hannah sings it thrills me so, they both are growing musically.

Church—This community is full of unforgiveness and grudge-holding to the point of being pandemic. My counseling load is picking up and it's mostly people from outside the church who used to attend here. Board is solid and helpful but there are still a lot of secrets I am discovering as I look through paperwork and board meeting notes. Feel a lot of motivation with the Body here, but also know that there is some pushback. Getting ready to deal with a series on sexual sin and hoping the church is ready. This is going to break some and push some over an edge they need to get over.

I have been here at Burkesville over nine years now, and have faced many challenges and experienced many victories. For the past several years, my medical life has been an interesting roller-coaster ride of shingles, anemia, sleep deprivation, and diabetic maintenance. In other areas of my life I have been very involved in the community, started on my doctoral degree, became a cat person because of my family (although two miniature schnauzers are part of the family now too), my son is now an Assemblies of God minister and my youth pastor (he got certified while he was a senior in high school), my eldest is finishing her Master of Arts at the University of Kentucky, and my youngest, at seventeen, is at NCU in Minneapolis.

My family grew up here in a pastor's home while I watched. My kids are older with a better understanding of the challenges of adulthood now, and they have a much better grip on how life works. You will see this a bit more in the following report that comes from January 2020:

Personal—Physical revelations this week as I discovered the blood work revealed a lot of irregularities—low serotonin, dopamine and epinephrine in serious decline. This was shocking to me and indicated that I also had a heart issue because of the sleep deprivation. They gave me several shots and I have slept for more than six hours for five nights in a row and feel overwhelmingly rested. I feel sharper and more focused than I have in many months. It is really like a second wind that even others have seen. My family especially. I have felt like I have been absent from my body for a while, and fragmented due to the stress of it all. I did not read one entire book in November which has never happened before. I have already read sixteen books this year and feel like my old self again in that regard. Temptations have been easier to fight as well, and thoughts have not been as dismal as they were. I felt exhausted at all times and the sleep therapists told me I was clinically depressed due to the lack of chemicals in my brain. She talked to me with bold strokes too as far my emotional health. She predicted a heart attack and a nervous breakdown if I went two more months like I was with sleep deprivation. I have thought and prayed much about this and see both the enemies hand and Gods provision over the last year. Most of my stress has been the personal financial strain and church finances. I paid out over $9,000 in medical bills out of a total income of $34,000 which is twenty-six percent of my income. This has hurt us deeply from where I was a year ago financially, but we have groceries every week and the bills are paid. The savings is gone because of the medical things, but I have a four-month supply of food set aside, stockpiling some bottled water, potable water, and a few other items in case things get interesting in America. Feel the need to prepare for difficulty so trying to be frugal and have enough for the family. Hannah has been to the ER close to the college twice this past week and even last night at 2am. She has not gotten over the sickness she had when she came home for break and is struggling. Also, last night a student at the university was found dead, and that has shaken her up a bit as she knew him. I have also looked at the billing website for our insurance and it looks like we are going to get billed for the entire deductible portion for Hannah, which is $2500 as her two visits to the ER were just under that amount (there are no clinics on campus and no urgent care places that take our insurance—just the local hospital). She is considered an adult at sixteen in Minnesota and not required to get permission for treatment. Will be calling the hospital tomorrow to see what kind of plan I can arrange to make payments. He has never let us down. Feel better physically and emotionally and seeing the fruit of that too.

Family—Jen is sick and not well but getting better, and we have had some good conversations about our kids this week and their outgrowth of us. Keilah is looking at apartments, and for a different job outside of our home town, and she is ready. She even asked me about a concealed carry class and getting a gun for protection (which makes this father happy). She has been buying some things and getting ready, and I have been praying for direction for her. Micah helped a young lady raise over $1,000 for STL (an Assemblies of God Youth missions fundraiser) as she took her birthday money and gave it to STL. He has set a goal of $20,000 for this year and is off to a great start. Talked about Hannah in the top part.

Church—Looking at a budget and getting solid direction for the finances, and feel much better. Having some real thoughts about another series on human sexuality and aiming it at teens and families (understanding temptations, not going along with the crowd, addressing the pornography epidemic, patterns for Christian dating and accountability).

Two of my board members in Burkesville are accountability partners and I have had as many as three of them as partners while here. Another accountability partner is my best friend in the world from back home in Indiana. He has been steadfast with me for many years. I also have a former board member and mentor from my home church in Indiana as a partner, as well as a friend from Texas who occasionally works in my community. One is an older pastor in my section of Assembly of God pastors who I have known for ten years and is like a father to me.

Since 1992 I have had over thirty accountability partners. Sadly, I could not share everything with some of these men because they talked to others too much. I have also had guys want to be a partner just because they were curious about what I was dealing with, and the struggles or sins I battled. The guys I have now are the best of the best partners I have ever had. Even though only one of the six regularly responds and tells me his life for the past week, I know they are all praying for me every week. What this tells you is accountability partnering may take some growing time, and experience to know what you need and what to look for.

What matters is when someone who knows you and knows your struggles is praying for you. It makes a huge difference.

I want to include one more of my accountability reports which

I had written a week before the last report I showed you. I want to show the week-to-week development of the situations and how much can change emotionally and relationally in that time. We all have those moments where we want to quit or walk away, where we are discouraged and down. Then we get a second wind, a small victory, or a major league win. Often it takes longer but sometimes it happens within a week. What matters is when someone who knows you and knows your struggles is praying for you. It makes a huge difference.

Personal—I had an eye-opening week. It started out crummy and with frustrations. I have watched attendance and finances slip at the church and have also had my own personal health and financial issues on top of it. I paid over $7,000 out of pocket, and that is after the deductible was met in August. I have grumbled too much and sometimes been far too critical attempting to justify it, but God has humbled me. Let me explain. For the last four months, I have had general thoughts about quitting ministry several times a week. It was based on disappointments that kept hitting close to home and close to the church. I was physically averaging two hours and fifteen minutes a night since the end of August, which eventually impacted my mental status and emotions. The doctor told me I had brain waves revealing sleep deprivation, and that my blood work revealed deprivation. So, it was catching up to me in bad ways. I was also tested while watching a TV documentary, during conversation while sitting and standing, and was watched while doing work on a computer. I failed every test within seven minutes, so it means my concentration was miserable. It also means that cognition and brain waves were starting to send me into either a meltdown or an anxiety attack. Glad I did not get there. The last two weeks with the CPAP machine have helped me tremendously, and last night I got over six hours of sleep. Jen tells me that I am not jerking my legs as much and that my movement at night is the best it has been since I married her. I have seen concerts and movies sponsored by the church have terribly low numbers, almost to the point of embarrassment, so that had me down. I even refused to advertise our churches showing of *Overcomer* this past Friday night. For New Year's Eve activity, we only had about ten people show up and I was really disappointed to a new low.

After most everybody had left, I started to walk out and just said to God, "Not doing this next year, and forget any holiday service at Christmas or New Year's Eve," and just had a complaining fit for a few minutes. Walked back in to the sanctuary, stood in the pulpit and asked God if I was done here because attendance is down, finances are down, nobody comes to many of the things that had been well attended in the past. Then my back tooth had a sharp pain that was like an ice pick being shoved in my mouth, but I heard nothing from God, nothing. So, I left again and got about forty feet outside the door walking home to the parsonage when I was impressed to stop, almost audibly, all this after saying, "And now my tooth hurts," out loud with attitude. Now the last forty feet had been a complaint marathon that I would be embarrassed for anyone to have heard, but God told me to stop and look up. I was impressed with "What do you see" so I said stars. "And who made them," and I said "You, God." "Why did I make them..." resulted in me stating scientific facts, and that it was evidence for God for everyone to see. The He said, "What if I made them just for you for tonight to see Me so you would stop complaining?" I then saw in my spirit a hand squeezing me and I was resisting and trying to get out, but it was Gods hand and there was no loosening of the grip. Then I heard in my spirit that the last year was to squeeze the things out of me that had to go, and I was almost done. So I got down on my knees at 11:34pm on New Year's Eve and repented of complaining and stressing over all of the personal and church problems. As I got up, I heard the word "Fifty" and "Discovery," so I prayed on that for several days, and Saturday a plan became clear. Starting today and for fifty days until Thursday February 20, I am to read out loud and slowly three chapters of the Word daily in the altar area of the sanctuary, and pray for three specific things: family, church, and nation. In the movie *Overcomer*, the star began to read Ephesians and write down what God said about her, so I knew that was the book to start reading out loud from. By the way, the movie had more people there than we had ever had at a movie, so God got my attention there too, plus I had not advertised it at all except on Facebook. I shared this story this morning with transparency and asked whosoever would to join me in reading out loud three chapters a day and praying for thirty minutes for

103

family, church, and nation. I will read and pray more than that personally, but the church will benefit even more at the altar time for healing if more are involved. I have felt an absolute second wind since sharing with the church this morning, and even took the service a different direction with the preaching, which ended up in a necessary prayer time for a woman dealing with pain. I was given a word of knowledge about loneliness and a lady responded with weeping, and many ladies came together to minister to her. The weight that I had carried into the church at 7:00am got much lighter and my spirit feels a bit more free. I am trusting God for help with my finances and family, for miracles of healings at Living Word Ministries church , and for growth and finances there as well, and within the fifty days' timeframe. I have a real calm that I have not felt since my brother's death and the financial blessing he gave to our family members. Trusting God for some big things in the next fifty days.

Family—Hannah went back to NCU driving for twelve straight hours to get there. She is considering staying over the summer and taking several classes. She was on the dean's list and incredibly, could graduate next Christmas after only one semester of college and graduating high school early less than seven months ago. We are finding out about housing possibilities and how many classes she can take, and if she will have financial aid for it. She can work at her job this summer and make some really good money, but she will be getting ahead as well. She could graduate college at nineteen which is rather cool to me. Proud of my youngest and her drive. Micah just turned his licensing paperwork in and is making decisions about where to finish his BA through. Hoping to know soon on this. Praying a lot for his relationship with his girlfriend, and for timing to be good with any decisions he makes in that regards. We are talking a lot about future for both of us, and what God is saying about what needs to be done immediately. Keilah is more set on moving out by the end of the summer as she finishes her MA and is starting to get restless, and it is honestly good timing for everybody. She is mature and responsible and will be successful in whatever she does. She is my oldest and has made me so proud over the years. She has a stubborn streak too, but it has been a good thing more often than not. Jen and I have also had a good week and she seems calmer since the holidays are over. She is sleeping better because I am sleeping better, and that has made a bigger difference than I imagined. We are both aging and it is obvious, but she is the love of my life and I am thankful for the last twenty-five and a half years together.

Church—I felt a second wind for the church today and am believing for miracles at the altar and financial gain in the next fifty days.

You can see from my accountability reports there are some things that have not changed and some areas that have simply developed and branched out. I can see eventual additions to my reports such as grandchildren, physical concerns for my wife and me, and other academic pursuits because of my love for learning. Part of the blessing of accountability is being able to forecast for the future, but to be really successful you have to be accountable for those parts of your life where you struggle. You then need to address those struggles often with your partners. You and only you determine what it looks like but you need to develop a pattern where you share the times you struggled during the week.

You will determine what details you share and the degree of honesty and transparency in your reports. If you hide your sins and negative tendencies so no one else knows what you struggle with, then you will fight alone even while you have people who are willing to fight for you. Share your victories too but share for the help you will receive in prayer.

I showed you my reports so you can see exactly what I share, and as you now know it's not always sin and temptations. Sometimes it is my emotional state or the weight of financial concerns. It might be specific issues with specific people, or a group issue. The bottom line is we all need someone looking out for us at all times, even as we get older. I believe this more and more as new uncharted territory is discovered in adulthood.

Now that we know what accountability looks like on paper, let's get to the real stuff. In the following chapters we will look at some of the biggest temptations we face.

Chapter Twelve

Your Greatest Temptations, Part I: Sexual Lust

Scattered throughout my office are various treasures from my childhood, my travels, and from friends around the world. Among these are a four pound chunk of the Berlin wall I broke off in July of 1990, a pineapple grenade shell from the Korean War brought home by an uncle, a Russian nesting doll I bought in Moscow, a solidarity pin I acquired in Gdansk, Poland, an arm-band worn by an actual Jewish captive from the Warsaw Ghetto, my Emmaus walk cross, a giraffe figurine from a missionary friend in Africa, and a Roman spear tip and flogging device made with accuracy to match the time of Christ by one of my accountability partners. I have many other interesting pieces but this gives you an idea of the eclectic nature of what I consider to have value.

I also have four bonsai trees I tend, over 1,800 books, a myriad of novelty puzzles and brainteasers, and lots of pictures of my wife, kids, and my miniature schnauzers—Moose and Mocha. Among these items is a military flag case holding the flag that rested on my father's casket the day he was buried. All these things have meaning to me but across different levels. The flag specifically reminds me of my father's service and the love he instilled in me for Old Glory and this great country. I can look at it and remember the discussions we had about the Vietnam War, about politics, and about government overreach. I also remember the hard times when he was drinking way too much and not around us a lot. These memories are sometimes rich and full of holes at other times, but they tie me to something I no longer have—access to my father.

The metaphor here is that accountability ties you to someone, and that connection endures and keeps you moored—being connected stops you from floating out to sea. Accountability keeps you from a Hansel and Gretel situation where the breadcrumbs disappear and you can't find your way back. Like my various treasures, accountability serves as a landmark to connect you to what is important. It means you have a plan and have people along the way to help you stay on the straight and narrow path and remain safe, because the breadcrumbs can be eaten by anything crossing your path. Worse, you can even choose to ignore your own breadcrumbs.

Accountability serves as a landmark to connect you to what is important.

Keeping your walk steady takes work, and it is more than a one-man or one-woman job. In modern life there are plenty of distractions to keep your eyes anywhere except on your steps and watching for the dangers along the way. In this chapter and the next, I would like to talk about two of the major struggles I have come across for men primarily, but increasingly for women in this day and age.

Lust and Pornography

Any guy who tells you his eyes never wander or that he is never tempted sexually is not just unusual, he is lying. Even if a man *has* managed to overcome these temptations to date, it does not mean he handles them perfectly every time, knowing how to avert his eyes or avoid them all together. It is a constant fight. We are human, we are part flesh, we are tempted—this is mankind in a nutshell. We live, work, and breathe in a sex-obsessed society that has become saturated to level of epidemic proportion since the birth of internet. It is ridiculously easy for temptation to find us, so up front we have to state the obvious: the mind of men is under attack. This daily reality was even made clear by Jesus Himself when He stated, "You have heard that it was said, 'You shall not commit adultery'; [28] but I say to you that everyone who looks at a woman with lust for her

Everyone who looks at a woman with lust for her has already committed adultery with her in his heart.

has already committed adultery with her in his heart" (Matthew 5:27-28, ESV).

Those are some heavy words but allow me to provide some insight into our Lord's statement. The act of adultery involves emotional *and* physical commitments, ignoring both boundaries and conscience. In the verse above, we are told that even the *thought* of sexual activity with a woman other than your wife is equal to adultery itself, a sinful and destructive act. Adultery is clear by the usage of the word but the idea here is that anyone looking at a woman with lust in his heart is where the line is drawn. The look that lingers longer than it should is sinful and wrong because *the thought seed becomes a potential for action*. This kind of gaze always prompts a thirst for more because the thought wishes to be more than just a thought; it wants to be

The thought seed becomes a potential for action.

fulfilled. Scripture itself is very clear about the power of sexual sin as the following passage reflects:

> [9] Or do you not know that the unrighteous will not inherit the kingdom of God? Do not be deceived; neither fornicators, nor idolaters, nor adulterers, nor effeminate, nor homosexuals, [10] nor thieves, nor *the* covetous, nor drunkards, nor revilers, nor swindlers, will inherit the kingdom of God. [11] Such were some of you; but you were washed, but you were sanctified, but you were justified in the name of the Lord Jesus Christ and in the Spirit of our God.
>
> [12] All things are lawful for me, but not all things are profitable.

All things are lawful for me, but I will not be mastered by anything. [13] Food is for the stomach and the stomach is for food, but God will do away with both of them. Yet the body is not for immorality, but for the Lord, and the Lord is for the body. [14] Now God has not only raised the Lord, but will also raise us up through His power. [15] Do you not know that your bodies are members of Christ? Shall I then take away the members of Christ and make them members of a prostitute? May it never be! [16] Or do you not know that the one who joins himself to a prostitute is one body *with her*? For He says, "The two shall become one flesh." [17] But the one who joins himself to the Lord is one spirit *with Him*. [18] Flee immorality. Every *other* sin that a man commits is outside the body, but the immoral man sins against his own body. [19] Or do you not know that your body is a temple of the Holy Spirit who is in you, whom you have from God, and that you are not your own? [20] For you have been bought with a price: therefore, glorify God in your body." 1 Corinthians 6:9-20 (NASB)

We can therefore conclude that lust needs to be addressed by every man for some serious reasons. The Center for Bible Engagement did a research brief in September 2013[20] on men and their spiritual struggles. The brief found that pornography's impact on men is devastating:

- Temptations to use pornography occur more times a day [than other temptations,] and men with this temptation spend more time thinking about it than other temptations.

- The temptation of lust and high rates of pornography use are also associated with more feelings of hopelessness and bitterness, feeling like you need to hide from others, feeling unable to please, and experiencing spiritual stagnation.

- Men who do not engage scripture regularly and do not have someone who holds them accountable have the highest rates of pornography use at 42%.

One great hope revealed from their research is that men who regularly engage scripture are 59% less likely to view pornography. Add accountability to the mix and it lowers the risk of viewing porn even more.[21] So, evidence suggests that while sexual lust is intensified by pornography and tempts all men of all ages, the challenge of this universal temptation is greatly reduced by spending time in the Word and being accountable to others.

I also believe that every man likely remembers their first glimpse of nudity or porn, where they were, and what they saw. This reminds me of something a pastor friend said one time, "It's easier to hang pictures up inside your head, than to remove them from the wall on which they hung." Reducing the amount of "pictures hung" is accomplished more easily with the help of a friend.

It is a fact that men are frequently being tempted by sexual lust, so we *must* understand the gravity of these spiritually destructive temptations. We as men must acknowledge daily that the enemy is *always* at the gate. These unrelenting, vicious forces are aimed at the purity of the mind, desiring to poison and dilute the soul. Christian men are equally impacted by these temptations, yet we avoid the discussion or even a casual conversation on the topic. In a different report titled "Christian Men & the Temptation of Pornography"[22] conducted by the Center for Bible Engagement another startling find was made; one that speaks directly to the issue at hand.

- Men who frequently attend church services still struggle with pornography, with estimates ranging from 33% to 63% engaging in it at least every few weeks.

- Men engaging in pornography also struggle more frequently with anger, hopelessness, and feeling like they have to hide.

The struggle with self-anger over viewing pornography is another big deal for men. Many of the men I have counseled who are struggling with sexual temptation, deal with a great amount of anger at themselves. For those struggling with sexual addictions, failures in self-control lead to anger when repeatedly going back to viewing these images and videos. The guilt and remorse they feel then leads to more anger. It becomes an increasingly bigger ship to steer, and the seas become stormier.

There is a large list of books, websites, and online resources on sexual addiction, pornography, and help for men of all ages who struggle with these issues, but clearly they have limited success because the person can engage or disengage at any time. There is usually no consequence for relapsing. I believe the best way to address and overcome the addiction of sexual lust is to be accountable to someone. I have heard hundreds of confessions from teenagers, single guys, and married men about their pornography and sexual addictions, and our conversation was the first time they had told anyone. They shared stories of guilt and helplessness, fear of discovery, and the disappointment others had felt in them when they had been found out. If this sounds exaggerated or excessive, believe me, I cannot overstate how destructive sexual sin is.

Dr. Jack Hayford, former President of The International Church of the Foursquare Gospel, lists ten reasons why sex sins are worse than others in a resource[23] he produced years ago. All ten reasons are relevant to this book.

- Sexual sin stains the root of an individual's basic point of identity.

- Exploits the deepest aspects of our emotionality.

- Pollutes the fountainhead of our highest creativity.

- Produces guilt that cripples confidence in authority.

- Compromise the foundation of life's deepest human relationship.

- Exposes the risk of fathering an unsupported child.

- Increases the probability of spreading disease.

- Gives place to appetites which provoke further unnatural behaviors.

- Breaches trust with the Body of Christ.

- Assaults the pure lordship of Christ in your life.

In my counseling and accountability experience, all of these issues become very apparent when confessions are made, or when discovery reveals the extent this sin has had on the person's life.

Every one of these points reflect the severe consequences of sexual sin and addiction in that arena. Statistical evidence proves it traumatizes the soul, destroys innocence, and muddies the conscience with debilitating guilt and shame. Sexual sin truly pollutes our vision, our mental faculties, poisons our position in Christ, and hinders the calling on our lives. The worst part is sexual sin is *never* satisfied, and feeding it simply causes a greater thirst for more, as it slowly burns a hole in the physical container succumbing to it.

These temptations are unrelenting and supremely destructive to the good within us, but they also infect our thoughts and our intentions. They cut us off from righteousness and barricade the path to holiness. When sexual sin has control in our lives, we find ourselves in a world of pain and shame and before we know it our lives are a total mess, often with lifelong consequences. Sexual sin affects more than just the individual, and for this reason it has to be confronted.

Sexual sin affects more than just the individual.

One volunteer firefighter confessed he had been called out to a fire the night before and had hurriedly shut his laptop, running out to work the fire. When his wife entered the home office she heard the computer humming and opened it to turn it off. What she saw on the screen stunned her. Gathering herself, she checked the browser history and made a copy. When he returned from work the next day his wife confronted him with the evidence. He was shocked and horrified to say the least. She told him she had opened every page he had visited and made it no secret she was more than disgusted in him as a husband and as a man. She read him the riot act. Consequently, for the following six weeks she monitored his phone and his computer usage. The man was humiliated, isolated, and temporarily estranged from his wife as she struggled to understand why he had been viewing pornography. He was broken.

I share this story because it is just one of countless I have heard, and it confirms the need for accountability. Eventually sexual sin always catches up to you. I have personally installed porn blocking software on my computer, shared my browsing history on a weekly basis, and even had a board member check my history on the computer itself once a week. All of these tools have helped me put up a security fence for my eyes and for my conscience.

The fireman in the story had struggled with pornography since high school and never told another living soul about it. He fought it by himself, regretted it by himself, and hated himself because he never told anyone until he got caught. At the time I was their pastor and just before she confronted him, his wife came by the church office to see me. She sobbed and wept for an hour, questioning what was wrong with him. She paced the office and shouted, wondering if she should divorce him and set his truck on fire (I'm not kidding).

I volunteered to hold him accountable and was able to calm her down, but she was broken by what she had discovered. She felt ugly and betrayed because he was looking at women who did not look like her, doing things that she would never do. She saw his fantasy life as superior and more important to him than his real life with her. You can't blame her for her reaction because what she believed of her relationship life had just taken a nose-dive as a naïve illusion.

Sexual sin blindsides those who discover it in their spouse, and brings out the worst emotions and disgust imaginable. I have mentioned that my pastoral ministry has followed moral failures in some of the churches I shepherded (which is a book on its own), and I have seen the wake of agony left for those who discover their leader was a hypocrite. Many fathers, sons, pastors, bankers, the poor, and the wealthy have walked into this trap and never managed to get out, but every one of them got away with it for a season. It always catches up to you but do you know what's better than getting caught? Having nothing to hide. A clean conscience is an indescribably precious possession that completely liberates a man from the terrible burden of guilt and shame.

Sometimes, however, when someone is caught there is the temptation to not confess all, or not to the full extent of what has been done. A study in a psychology journal in 2014[24] indicated the following to be true:

"Confessions are people's way of coming clean, sharing unethical acts with others. Although confessions are traditionally viewed as categorical—one either comes clean or not—people often confess to only part of their transgression. Such partial confessions may seem attractive, because they offer an opportunity to relieve one's guilt without having to own up to the full consequences of the transgression. In this article, we explored the occurrence, antecedents, consequences, and everyday prevalence of partial confessions. Using a novel experimental design, we found a high frequency of partial confessions, especially among people cheating to the full extent possible. People found partial confessions attractive because they (correctly) expected partial confessions to be more believable than not confessing. People failed, however, to anticipate the emotional costs associated with partially confessing. In fact, partial confessions made people feel worse than not confessing or fully confessing, a finding corroborated in a laboratory setting as well as in a study assessing people's everyday confessions. It seems that although partial confessions seem attractive, they come at an emotional cost."

The study tells us less is definitely not more in this scenario and confessing to half of what you did is not what God requires nor expects. Confessing your sins one to another and praying for each other's healing is what James suggests in James 5:16, and these two work together like peas and carrots. Confessing your sins to someone else not only sheds the burden of guilt, it gains that person's prayers concerning what you confessed. It brings someone else into the

Confessing your sins to someone else not only sheds the burden of guilt, it gains that person's prayers.

fight you have been fighting alone, and let's face it, sexual temptation is something we will all face again in the very near future. It is an extremely difficult, if not impossible, fight to win without help so don't for another minute continue alone, fighting one of the biggest battles you will consistently face.

In closing this chapter, I understand human sexuality is a taboo subject among most human beings. I know even Christian parents are leery to talk to their kids or teens about the topic of sex, and in the

If this topic is not discussed, we are failing to pass on biblical truths to the generations to come.

secular world where kids don't have a biblical grounding the impact of silence is worse. These children learn about sex from movies, pornography, or friends who have never talked to a parent about the topic either. We have many justifications as to why we don't broach the subject, but history and the current social mess should

be enough evidence to suggest that we had better start discussing it. The fall of man ruined a great plan God had for humanity and sexuality in the context of marriage. If this topic is not discussed, we are failing to pass on biblical truths to the generations to come.

In Job 31:1, Job declares he had made a covenant with his eyes, so how could he look at a virgin. The statement implies he understood lust to be a common temptation among men. He made the covenant with God, meaning he confessed his temptations to the Lord and knew how much he needed help in fighting them. He called upon the Lord because he knew where his strength would come from. By making his story public, Job was not only admitting to a tendency, but revealing the secret to overcoming it. He knew the one, true God who would help when called upon. Job humbly admitted his need in this arena and God faithfully answered his plea. If we are to overcome this gravely destructive sin, we should do the same and expect the same from God.

In the next chapter, we will uncover the other major temptation men face in their spiritual and everyday walk. It is a sin we touched on in this chapter, but will explore in more detail in the next.

Chapter Thirteen

Your Greatest Temptations, Part II: Anger

I know why I have dealt with overwhelming anger throughout my past. I was a small kid, constantly bullied by bigger kids, and embarrassed by my father's drunkenness, and the poverty in which I was raised. In the early seventies my father had a business making good money but he had lost it all by the time I left elementary school. Suddenly the nice things we had were gone, the quality of life we enjoyed changed abruptly, and embarrassment and bullying began to fuel a smoldering anger.

Before he died, my dad told me that at one time he had $20,000 in a savings account for new cars for my brother and me when we turned sixteen. There was also $40,000 invested for our college funds, even though we were both younger than ten at that point. It was gone in a flash because of new business trends, and my brother and I did not even know we had it. When my dad eventually kicked the drinking and the related spending, we were left in the wake of the storm.

For the next three years, though, we had no income except for what my mom was paid to clean a few churches. She even got another job working nights, and some family members also helped us as much as they could. I started mowing yards at eleven years old and giving the money to my mom to help to pay the bills. Then my dad's alcoholism kicked into high gear and family fights became constant. As my hope of returning to our former life was slowly chipped away, anger seeped into those crevices and cracks like molten lava as I watched it all fall apart. Middle school became the hardest testing ground for me based on the clothes I wore, the free lunches I had to eat, the lack of money for field trips (or anything for that matter), and the angst of my future being a huge question mark based on my family's situation.

Soon I became no stranger to fights, vandalizing property, and on various occasions, I even found myself sitting in the back of police cars. All of it was due to a then-seething anger problem that had grown severely out-of-control. I was a kid ashamed by my family conditions and acting out every chance I got. A heavy bag hanging in the garage and a pair boxing gloves were exhausted as I acted out revenge fantasies of punching and kicking the people I felt had robbed me of something. I never drank nor took drugs but violence became a part of my young life, taking root in my pain.

This pain and subsequent violence began even while my dad still had his business. From kindergarten to second grade I was tormented on the school bus by three middle school kids. Several times a week I was held down by those bigger boys as they lit a stick match and touched it to my neck. At first I made a lot of noise but was quickly threatened to keep quiet or they would hurt my younger brother. As much as it hurt physically, it enraged me even more.

I never drank nor took drugs but violence became a part of my young life, taking root in my pain.

This took place almost daily for three long years on that bus. Sometimes the match was only lit as they cackled, threatening to burn me, but often they blew it out and put the searing tip to my neck. I never told a soul and refused to shed any tears except when I couldn't take the agony. I never cried after each incident, but I was tormented mentally. Daily I dreamed of revenge on those three guys who burned me.

Eventually I got hold of a karate book and started practicing on that bag, focusing every ounce of rage into each punch and kick. Still, I was in the seventh grade before I hit 100 lbs. and was just five feet tall until my freshmen year, so make no mistake, I had no physical advantages at all. As I said, my dad had the business and was still doing well, and his store was in a much bigger community so there was a karate dojo only two blocks away. At the end of the second grade I decided to move from the heavy bag, and took advantage of the dojo all during the summer.

All I need to tell you is when I got back on the bus as a third grader I was angry, trained, and more than ready for revenge. I succeeded to the point that I spent my first minutes off the bus in the Principal's office for my alleged abuse of the guys who had been hurting me for the previous three years. I will also tell you, however, that they never hurt me again, never even touched me in fact, and never teased me again either.

I have only recently revealed the bullying I took on that bus. I never told the bus driver, nor the school, nor my family. I was embarrassed, ashamed, and afraid, but after three years I'd had enough and was not going to take it anymore. In one way I see it as a "good scar" from my childhood because it built into me a confidence that was not there before. It also, however, cut a deep, angry channel in my heart which I would wrestle with for decades. To this day, I sometimes feel it come rushing to the top when I see or experience an injustice. I also still have the white scar on my neck where the glowing match heads were placed to remind me of that period in my life.

It also, however, cut a deep, angry channel in my heart which I would wrestle with for decades.

Anger is more often a man's problem, which is why men fight more, argue more, and demand more, at least in my opinion. Still, anger is sometimes unavoidable. Ephesians 4:26-27 (NASB,) says

"²⁶ Be angry, and yet do not sin; do not let the sun go down on your anger, ²⁷ and do not give the devil an opportunity." Anger is an emotion that is always supposed to be kept in check. Somewhat like a firearm, this verse means anger should be registered and holstered, but never allowed to be brandished or used beyond certain lines. We are allowed to be angry, upset, perturbed, and flat-out mad, but we are *never* granted any permission to express it in an unholy manner. Once we step over the line our Christian witness is blown; the crowd sees our carelessness. We have allowed raw emotion to control us and the way we are subsequently viewed by others is then marred. Even holding on to anger through the night is prohibited because the longer you hold it, the heavier it gets, and the more determined you will be to do something you will regret. In this way, as the verse says, you will be giving the devil an opportunity in your life.

Proverbs 15:1 (ESV) says, "A soft answer turns away wrath, but a harsh word stirs up anger." After church one Wednesday night I was driving some kids home in the church van when a father, high on drugs, accused me of driving way too fast. In reality I was parked in his driveway. He approached the stationary van and began cursing and screaming at me to stop going so fast. He was waving a bottle around, talking about beating on me, and just acting like a maniac. Blindsided by this sudden outburst, that anger flashed up in my chest but I knew the kids in the van were watching this play out. I rolled down the window, but I was concerned—more for the kids—about what the nut might do.

He stomped right up to the window screaming as loudly as he could but I took a breath and very softly just said, "I can do that, sir." He could not hear me so I said it softer, "I can do that, sir."

He finally got quiet and leaned in and softly said, "What?"

I quietly repeated myself again, "I can do that, sir."

"All right then," he said in a normal voice, stood up, turned around, and walked back into the house without any show of force or stupidity.

The kids then explained that the father had also yelled at the van driver who had picked them up before church because the driver had been running late after work. I now had a better picture of why he was yelling, but he made an assumption it was me driving too fast earlier. What if I had made a scene? I was the youth pastor with a van full of impressionable kids who had a certain idea of the kind of person I was. If I had started screaming back at the guy, there is zero doubt it would have resulted in a fight. Instead, the kids talked about that event for months and I had an object lesson for a gentle answer turning away wrath for years to come. That is a huge win.

The bottom line is losing your temper anywhere is bad news. Proverbs 25:28 (ESV) says, "A man without self-control is like a city broken into and left without walls." Control your anger and you will control so much more than just your fists. It helps the mind to think intelligent, right thoughts, the mouth to use wise words, and the blood pressure to normalize.

Anger is a topic that needs to not only be addressed but prioritized in accountability sessions. We need to be held accountable by others to the point that, sometimes, there is even the need for our partners to force accountability so we and others stay safe. I played little league baseball as a kid and one of the boys on my team had a father who was friends with my dad. One night after a game, the guy's wife drove to the ballpark and asked where

A man without self-control is like a city broken into and left without walls.

my dad was. She was quite a sight—I could tell she had been crying, and had fresh, swollen bruising around her eye. I asked if she was okay and she smiled weakly and again asked where my dad was. I pointed to the car where he was sitting and she went and talked to him. After about fifteen minutes she left but her son came home with us that night without any explanation from my dad or the kid's mom.

This took place in summer and we already had a six-person tent already set up in the back yard, so we decided my brother and I, and the other kid, would bunk out there. We cooked hot dogs over a fire, talked about all kinds of kid stuff, and gazed at the stars for hours before we were settled enough to go to bed. We had just arranged the sleeping area with sleeping bags, pillows, and blankets when the kid revealed something that struck me like lightning: "My dad gets drunk and beats my mom and me, and when I go home with somebody else, I worry he will kill her." Just like that, he blurted it out and then was quiet. I was stunned. For a few moments I was awkwardly silent but eventually I managed to ask what he meant, because I had a dad who got drunk but he never beat on us or our mom. He didn't say anything more. He just rolled over in the safety of our tent, two miles from his house, and slept.

Years later I asked my dad about the situation. He told me that basically the lady had talked to him several times before and told him her husband would get violent when he drank. Since he and my dad drank together, she was hoping he could help her husband tone it down and keep him from going too far. For the most part my dad did help, but the guy figured out what was going on and he eventually stopped drinking with my dad. That night her husband had shown up after work in a very violent mood and asked where his son was. She explained that he was playing ball but he didn't believe her so he punched her. She ran and hid in a bedroom but he tried to tear the door down so she climbed out of a window and drove into town to ask someone to hide her son for the night. She went to my dad first and he came through for her. He didn't say a word about the situation, he just did the right thing and kept a kid from getting hurt. He also gave her thirty dollars to stay in a hotel that night so she would be safe too.

I will never know how much trouble my dad helped spare that mom and her son, but that kid spent the night with us about ten times that summer and we became good friends. He never mentioned his dad or being beaten again while in our home or in the tent outside. Then, before school started that fall they were gone and I have never seen nor heard from him since. My dad later revealed that the mother divorced the father, got full custody of the son, a protective order against the father, and then left the state. The woman had trusted my dad, but even more than that, she needed my dad to help her be accountable for the safety of her son. I was a kid who could not help the people involved in any meaningful way even if I had known the situation, but looking back I am really glad my dad helped.

The point is if you don't deal with anger issues, chances are you know someone who does, so I encourage you to step in and keep them accountable. If you do struggle with anger, you must confess that to someone and start being accountable for your actions and words, because unbridled anger never leads anybody to a good place. James 1:19-20 (NASB 1995) says, "[19] You know this, my beloved brethren. But everyone must be quick to hear, slow to speak *and* slow to anger; [20] for the anger of man does not achieve the righteousness of God." Our anger cannot change situations, people, or history, and it especially will not work for us in overcoming an addiction or struggle either. Unchecked anger cannot change a thing except to make matters worse. If I get mad about my sin and act out with words or actions, then feel tremendous guilt after making a fool of myself, I still have done nothing to help the issue, and have actually made it worse.

The verse referenced above makes it clear that getting angry at our sin is not enough to change the behavior—we *must* have self-control, and self-control is very difficult to achieve without the Spirit of God working in us. The apostle Paul addressed anger enough that I strongly suspect he had moments of becoming unhinged himself, especially before he knew Jesus. He was, after all, a Pharisee of Pharisees, proud of his

Getting angry at our sin is not enough to change the behavior—we must have self-control.

ancestry, and respected by the religious leaders of the Jewish people. In Colossians 3:8 (NASB 1995) he made the following statement, "But now you also, put them all aside: anger, wrath, malice, slander, *and* abusive speech from your mouth." I want you to notice how anger builds up to wrath, then to malice, then to slander and abusive speech. These are all rooted in the anger that started it all. Anger always starts badly, and ends even worse.

Self-control on the other hand is one of the fruits of the Spirit and that is a gift that we, as men, need to pursue in a very determined way. Learning to control anger is admittedly a tremendous challenge, especially if there was not a good example we observed when we were growing up. Regardless of our past, however, we are compelled by scripture to live a life worthy of Jesus' holy name. This is exactly why accountability, transparency, and honesty are so important and necessary to our lives. Our refusal to pursue these disciplines will ultimately bring chaos to our families because our untold secrets will be controlling our actions. Even worse, we will never admit that we know this is true. If you struggle with anger, believe me, everybody knows it regardless of whether or not you have ever admitted it. Other people often see clearly what we won't see or admit about ourselves. Admitting it now and pursuing self-control will save you a great deal of trouble later in life, and that is the real focus and intention of accountability. It keeps you safe, and it keeps others safe too.

Sexual sin and anger are such devastating plagues to the soul and spiritual health of every man. Spiritual maintenance therefore becomes a daily necessity. The Christian can go to church every time the doors open but still have a very hollow soul. Without consistent Bible study, time in prayer, fellowship, and accountability, there are pieces missing that will always stifle victory in the many battles we face each week. Every piece is important. Like cogs in a machine, each piece impacts how the others work, the precision in which they operate, and even the speed of how they work.

These two great sins are stronger than ever in today's society, which is why we need to publicly address them and privately be accountable for them.

Chapter Fourteen
Putting It All Together

We now know what accountability is, why we need accountability and transparency in our lives, the type of accountability partners we need, and how to identify and select them. From a practical perspective, we covered what transparency will cost you, what accountability looks like in practice, and highlighted our biggest temptations as men. It's now time to wrap it all up and put the plan into action.

By this point, I trust that you have considered your own life, the mistakes you have made, your victories, and the friends who might be willing to assist in holding you accountable. I hope you found the stories I shared interesting, but more so that they moved you to action regarding the point I was trying to convey in each chapter. Your life and mine are distinct testaments consisting of a lifetime of individual stories, and our minds are filled with memories and images from the decades of experiences we have lived through. We have regrets and recollections we wish we did not have, but many aspects of life have no do-overs or second chances, so we are left living with the consequences of the choices we made. Sharing these stories provides the opportunity to help change the course of many other lives if they are willing learn from us regarding both the good and the bad consequences of our choices. Revelation 12:11a (NASB) says "And they overcame him because of the blood of the Lamb and because of the word of their testimony..." which partially sums up the power of accountability. So get ready to tell your story—your weaknesses, vulnerabilities, and your victories included—but tell your story to someone and tell it loudly.

Let me share one more story that makes sense to include here at the end: a lady in one of the churches I pastored began to experience dementia and issues related to memory loss. She was an exceptionally sweet lady, but when the condition overcame her she sometimes became very hostile and mean-spirited. It was not her fault so it would simply not have been fair to get upset with her. I felt for her every time I visited her, whether at home, in the nursing home, or in the hospital.

Her first steps toward dementia began gradually with no indication of how severe it would suddenly become. During the early stages of her condition she was sometimes hospitalized, spending over a week there on one occasion. I went to see her the day she was admitted and we talked a bit, then I prayed with her before leaving. When I returned to see her next day, though, she thought she had been there for five days and that I had not been to see her in all that time. She did not seem her usual self so I shook it off and explained that she had been admitted the previous day, and that I had been to see her the same day.

Suddenly she began cursing and swearing, and screaming at me. I knew her past, and that she had probably never spoken a curse word in her entire life, but she was so livid the nurse had to come in to calm her down. After the nurse got her settled I asked a family member who had arrived in the middle of the lady's episode what was going on with her. She explained the preliminary diagnosis of dementia and Alzheimer's disease, and that it had come on suddenly after a very small stroke (which is why she was hospitalized to begin with).

On my return the following day I met the same nurse I had spoken with and asked how the lady was feeling. I was told she was sharp as a tack that day. I pulled out one of my business cards and asked her to put the two dates I had previously been to see the lady on the back of the card and to include that day's date. I then asked her to put her initial beside each date. The nurse asked me why I requested she do this. I told her it was to record that I had been there, regardless of whether the patient remembered my visit or not. Once she had initialed the card I entered the ward, and after talking to the lady for about thirty minutes I prayed with her and left the card on the night stand. I returned two days later to a complaint from the lady that I had not been in to see her at all. I told her to watch me walk over and fetch the card from the night stand then asked her to read it with me. We checked the three dates, the initials of the nurse against the date, and the name of the nurse on duty listed on the marker board up in the ward. The lady began crying and apologized for not believing me. I had the card initialed again that day, but took it with me that time.

I came back five more times to see her for a total of eight times in ten days, but she only remembered me being there once. The point is I had the eight days I was there initialed by a nurse to confirm to the patient that I had been to see her. She was still upset each time that I had not been to visit, but there was accountability when the nurse and family members confirmed I had been there. You see, I had a nurse help me be accountable to someone who would not even remember anything of her day, let alone whether I had been there or not.

My point is accountability matters for conscience sake—yours and the other person's. We do a lot of living when no one is watching. I mean, really think about how much of your time daily is spent entirely and absolutely alone. There are times when no one is with you except the Spirit of God, your critical thinking skills, and your absolute will to stay holy. Accountability removes the possibility of straying from the path when no one is around to witness your actions.

Accountability removes the possibility of straying from the path when no one is around to witness your actions.

I would like to reiterate, the process I covered in this book is merely the way *I* do accountability. You can make it to be whatever it needs to be to best serve you. The way I practice accountability may not work for you so craft your approach to the specifications you require to make it work. What matters at this point is that you do *something* to maintain accountability, and you keep doing it. It is never too late to start being accountable, even if you have never been accountable to anyone else in your lifetime. Starting the process is not that difficult, but setting it up will take a little bit of time and effort. You owe it to yourself and the people you love to take the first step towards changing your life for the better.

Four Practical Steps to Accountability

Getting back to our practical perspective, I assure you that if you follow these next four steps you will see a difference in your marriage, in your family, in your job, in your thoughts, and your church:

First step: Search your heart. Be honest with yourself before the Lord about your life, your sins, your addictions, and your secrets. Give some thought as to who you are in Christ, then truthfully weigh that up against who you are in real life. Who are you really, compared to what people see when you are in public? What do you hide from your wife and kids, or what would you be ashamed for others to know about you when in private? Have you ever asked God to search your heart to reveal to you anything contrary to His will in your life? If you are honest with God, and truly want to be accountable for your actions, make it a matter of prayer and he will reveal the areas in your life requiring refinement.

Second step: Find that person who will hold you accountable. This is someone who loves you but will be firm with you, brutally honest with you, and will get in your face if necessary. You need someone who will cut you no slack, yet show you plenty of grace and brotherly love when you need it. I also recommend a range of accountability partners, if possible. Try to find at least one or two people slightly older than you so you can tap into their wisdom, maturity, and battle experience. I also suggest partnering with someone close to your age as they will be experiencing similar temptations and life issues. If it is feasible, try to also find someone much younger than you so you can mentor them in the realm of accountability. Even if all you can find is just one other friend to partner with, get the accountability process going, regardless of their age or experience.

Third step: Identify what your accountability relationship will look like, how it will work, and then begin to establish patterns. Find an approach that works for both of you based on work schedules, family commitments, and general availability. Consistency is key so figure out what it takes to make consistent meeting times. Set the boundaries regarding when and how you will meet. Agree whether it will be a sit-down meeting or a weekly email blitz. Will you do it over breakfast, early in the morning before work, or after church on a Sunday afternoon? Discuss all the aspects of the partnership, and get it set so you can start as soon as possible. You will probably need to tweak the arrangement over the first couple of weeks and months, then polish it until it is a well-oiled machine. Just make sure it works for you and for your accountability partner, and it will be a game-changer for both of your lives.

Fourth step: Grow as a human being. This is the most important step—the reason for accountability and transparency. To grow spiritually and as a person you *must* learn from being held accountable for your areas of weakness. Accountability and sharing your secrets doesn't come naturally, so you need to learn how to be accountable, how to hold someone else accountable, and how to grow in *Don't expect perfection when you begin the process.* the grace and knowledge of Christ as you do. *Don't expect perfection when you begin the process.* It will take time to become honest with yourself and transparent with your partner. One week will be hit and miss and the next week a homerun. Just start being accountable, and perfect the way you do it on the journey.

You will never understand how powerful accountability and transparency is for your life until you try it. If doubts arise when making the decision to become accountable, ask yourself how confessing your weaknesses, your struggles, and your sins can not improve your spiritual life? How can a stronger spiritual life not impact your emotional health and physical well-being for the better? How can accountability not make a difference in your body, soul, and spirit and bring fulfillment as well? Speaking from experience I promise you it will, and after decades

129

of sharing my secrets and my soul, I am determined to continue doing so until I draw my last breath. I need accountability in my life because I know it makes me a better husband and a better father. I know it makes me a better pastor and greatly strengthens the example I set. It makes me a better friend, a better person, and a much better human being.

You may ask how I know this for sure. I know because for several decades now I have been getting outstanding results from sharing my secrets and my personal pain with several accountability partners. They, in turn, have prayed for me, held up my arms when I was under fire from spiritual darkness, and encouraged me in my walk with Jesus. I have totally defeated numerous enemies along the way, and am steadily chipping away at others. You see, some enemies take longer to destroy than others, but because of accountability, I have some significant victory notches on my belt. Therein lies the purpose of it; to emerge as an overcomer walking confidently in the light.

Consistent victory and progress is the reason we all need accountability. In Heaven we will be an open book, yet in Matthew 6:10 the Lord told us to bring Heaven to Earth. I propose that we can never effectively do this without accountability.

New levels of victory are waiting for you.

Please get started today. Take action right now and call the person (or people) you have already identified in your heart. If you wait, it will probably slip away to the bottom of your "to (never) do" list. New levels of victory are waiting for you, so why delay a moment longer?

May God's grace and richest blessings rest upon you.

Pastor Dana.

Endnotes

1   The American Heritage Dictionary 2nd College Edition. Boston: Houghton Mifflin Harcourt, 1982.

2   Ibid

3   Webster's Collegiate Thesaurus. Springfield, MA: Merriam-Webster, 1976.

4   Ibid

5   Fernandez, Colin. "Adulthood begins at 30: Scientists say that our brains are not fully grown-up in our twenties." Daily Mail Online. https://www.dailymail.co.uk/sciencetech/article-6824499/Adulthood-begins-30-Scientists-say-brains-not-fully-grown-twenties.html (accessed August 4, 2020).

6   The American Heritage Dictionary 2nd College Edition. Boston: Houghton Mifflin Harcourt, 1982.

7   Howard, J. Grant. The Trauma of Transparency. Oregon: Multnomah Press, 1979.

8   Transparency." Fine Dictionary. http://www.finedictionary.com/transparency.html (accessed November 23, 2020).

9   Ibid

10   James 5:16

11   Day, Martin V., and D. Ramona Bobocel. 2013. "The Weight of a Guilty Conscience: Subjective Body Weight as an Embodiment of Guilt." Edited by Manos Tsakiris. PLoS ONE 8, no. 7: e69546. https://doi.org/10.1371/journal.pone.0069546 (accessed May 27, 2021).

12   Winch, Guy (Ph.D.) "10 Things You Didn't Know About Guilt." Psychology Today. https://www.psychologytoday.com/intl/blog/the-squeaky-wheel/201411/10-things-you-didnt-know-about-guilt (accessed November 25, 2020).

13   ibid

14   "Reprove." Merriam-Webster. https://www.merriam-webster.com/dictionary/reprove (accessed November 26, 2020).

15   "Statistics for Pastors." n.d. Www.Pastoralcareinc.com. https://www.pastoralcareinc.com/statistics/ (accessed December 2, 2020).

16   Vitello, Paul. "Taking a Break From the Lord's Work (Published 2010)." The New York Times, August 2, 2010, sec. New York. https://www.nytimes.com/2010/08/02/nyregion/02burnout.html (accessed December 2, 2020).

17   "2017 Pastor Burnout Statistics | Pentecostal Theology." n.d. https://www.pentecostaltheology.com/2017-pastor-burnout-statistics/ (accessed December 3, 2020).

18   Anderer, John. "Perpetual Stress: Four In Ten Adults Close To 'Breaking Point' At Work." Study Finds. October 11, 2019. https://www.studyfinds.org/perpetual-stress-four-in-ten-adults-close-to-breaking-point-at-work/ (accessed December 3, 2020).

19   "OnePoll Market Research and PR Surveys | New York, California, London." OnePoll Research. https://www.onepoll.com/groupon-work-life-balance/ (accessed December 3, 2020).

20   Ovwigho, Pamela. Arnie Cole. "Center for Bible Engagement." The Devastating Effect of Losing Everyman's Battle – Spiritual Trends of our Sons, Brothers, Boyfriend's, Husbands & Dads, Research Brief. https://bttbfiles.com/web/docs/cbe/Spiritual_Crises_among_Men.pdf (accessed January 27, 2021).

21   Ibid.

22   Ovwigho, Pamela. Arnie Cole. "Center for Bible Engagement." Christian Men & the Temptation of Pornography Research Brief. https://bttbfiles.com/web/docs/cbe/Christian_Men_and_Pornography_Oct_2010.pdf (accessed January 27, 2021).

23   Hayford, Jack. Fatal Attractions, Why Sex Sins Are Worse Than Others. Raleigh NC: Regal Books, 2004.

24   Peer, E., Acquisti, A., & Shalvi, S. Review of "I Cheated, but Only a Little": Partial Confessions to Unethical Behavior. n.d. American Psychological Association. https://psycnet.apa.org/record/2014-02577-002 (accessed January 27, 2021).